Man Made God

Man Made God

THE MEANING OF LIFE

Luc Ferry

TRANSLATED BY DAVID PELLAUER

THE UNIVERSITY OF CHICAGO PRESS • CHICAGO AND LONDON

Luc Ferry teaches at the Sorbonne and at the University of Caen in France. He is the author or coauthor of seven previous books published by the University of Chicago Press, including most recently *The New Ecological Order*.

Originally published as Luc Ferry, *L'Homme-Dieu, ou Le Sens de la vie* (Paris: Grasset, 1996). © Éditions Grasset et Fasquelle, 1996.

The University of Chicago Press, Chicago 60637
The University of Chicago Press, Ltd., London
© 2002 by The University of Chicago
All rights reserved. Published 2002
Printed in the United States of America

11 10 09 08 07 06 05 04 03 02   1 2 3 4 5
ISBN: 0-226-24484-9 (cloth)
ISBN: 0-226-24485-7 (paper)

Library of Congress Cataloging-in-Publication Data
Ferry, Luc.
  [Homme-Dieu, ou, Le sens da la vie. English]
  Man made God: the meaning of life / Luc Ferry.
    p. cm.
  Includes bibliographical references and index.
  ISBN 0-226-24484-9 (cloth : alk. paper)—ISBN 0-226-24485-7 (pbk. : alk. paper)
    1. Life. 2. Humanism. I. Title.

BD435 .F4713 2001
128—dc21

                                                                    2001053001

∞ The paper used in this publication meets the minimum requirements of the American National Standard for Information Sciences—Permanence of Paper for Printed Library Materials, ANSI Z39.48-1992.

CONTENTS

The Meaning of Life

THE WITHDRAWAL OF A QUESTION

In the *Tibetan Book of Living and Dying* Sogyal Rinpoche recounts the story of Krisha Gotami, a young woman living during the time of the Buddha. A sudden illness carried off her one-year-old son. Overwhelmed with grief, holding her beloved child, Krisha wandered through the streets, imploring all those she met to show her a way of bringing him back to life. Some ignored her, others thought her mad, but finally a wise man advised her to speak to the Buddha. So she went to see him, laying the small corpse at his feet and telling him of her misfortune. The sage listened to her with an infinite compassion and gently told her, "There is just one way to heal your affliction. Go down to the town and bring me a mustard seed from any house where there has never been a death." [1]

We can guess the rest of the story. Its moral, too. Krisha knocked on all the doors, and each time she received the same answer: there would be no problem in giving her a mustard seed, but as for the rest, every house had its dead, none had escaped. When the young woman returned to the Buddha, she was already on the Way: nothing in our human world is permanent. The one eternal element is "impermanence" itself, the fluctuating and perishable quality of all things. Those foolish enough to not see this expose themselves to the worst kind of suffering, in all its forms.

But if we become aware of the true causes of evil, if we see that they stem from the illusions of an ego that clings to its "possessions" when the law of the world is change, we can begin to free ourselves. This is wisdom.

In their different ways, all great religions try to prepare human beings for death, their own as well as that of their loved ones.[2] It is in terms of this initiation that they invite us to decipher the meaning of human life. Even ancient ethical theories—those of the Stoics, for example, but closer to us also that of Montaigne—take it as certain that wisdom lies in the acceptance of an order of the world that includes finitude, so that to "philosophize" is to "learn to die." Numerous passages in the Gospels touch on this question—born from the conflict that opposes love, which leads to attachment, and death, which means separation—with a simplicity comparable to that of the Tibetan book. However different, the proposed answers are nonetheless all dictated by the concern to establish a tie between the end of life and its ultimate meaning. When Jesus learns of the death of Lazarus, he suffers just as other humans do. Like Martha and Mary, Lazarus's sisters, he begins to weep. But he already knows that he is going to give existence back to someone who never doubted, and he says to Martha: "I am the resurrection and the life. Those who believe in me, even though they die, will live, and everyone who lives and believes in me will never die" (John 11:25–26).

Should we learn to accept impermanence, or should we place our faith in the permanence of life? At first sight the opposition between them seems complete. But perhaps it conceals a more hidden affinity in that, for the Christian as for the Buddhist, the question of meaning comes to the fore in the face of finitude. For both, the wise person is the one who prepares himself by turning away from "having," from the attachments and possessions of this world, to the profit of "being." The logic of happiness is not the only one that counts. This is so true that in the eyes of believers, until recently, it went without saying that a long agony, however painful, was infinitely preferable to a quick end, however painless.[3] At least it left one time to make peace with oneself and to commend one's soul to God.

The Banality of Mourning

For us modern people, the significance of this attitude has bit by bit been lost sight of. Forearmed atheists or agnostics, we would prefer to die suddenly, with no suffering and, if possible, without having to think about it. To us all meditation on death seems superfluous, not really "virile," and in a word that sums it up, pathological. Freud, who was the thinker of disillusion par excellence, put it straightforwardly: When one begins to ask oneself questions about the meaning of life and death, one must be sick, for none of this has any objective existence. But were Montaigne and the Stoics neurotics? And with them, all the supposedly wise men of tradition? Maybe the scales of superstition have fallen from our eyes, but deprived of myths, what do we have left to say or think in the face of the absurdity of mourning? Psychology, it is a well-known fact, has dethroned theology. Yet on the day of burial, at the foot of the grave and the coffin, a certain discomfort takes hold of us. What are we to say to the mother who has lost her daughter, to the grief-stricken father? We are dramatically confronted with the question of meaning or, rather, with its eclipse in a secularized world. Reduced to the language of feeling, we inwardly feel its limits. Whatever comfort a few compassionate gestures may bring, however precious this is, it does not measure up to the question posed by an absence that we know well has become, in the strict sense of the word, meaningless. Whence the banalities one always hears. They do not, however, conceal that the king is naked. If the wisdom of the great religious traditions no longer fits our democratic times, if any turning back seems impossible, neither have we invented anything that can acceptably take their place. Without being completely useless, the crutches offered by psychoanalysis are only that: clever prostheses. Freud has defeated Montaigne, but his victory leaves a bitter taste.

The reason for this sense of emptiness is clear. From the perspective of religious eschatology, old age, far from being the sign of an irreversible and senseless decline, was, if not the synonym of wisdom, at least one of the necessary conditions for attaining it. It occupied an eminent, irreplaceable position among the ages of life.

The retinue of pains that accompanied it could be taken as a kind of initiation test—right where we see only a kind of absolute negativity. In a way exactly opposite to traditional teachings, we have even sometimes come to confer an ethical significance on euthanasia. The idea of messianic times was that there should "no longer be a man who did not reach the goal of his old age," whatever the price might be.[4] Our societies, by contrast, with their orientation toward the future, solidly committed to "progress," have very little to say about these aches and pains except that, in the face of them, the one thing to do is find a way to escape.

As regards this radical change in our relation to meaning, there is one motif that Rousseau, a precursor of our disenchanted times on this point as on so many others, had already caught sight of in an insightful passage from his *Discourse on the Origins of Inequality*. In his eyes it is the very essence of "modern" people, marking their difference from the animals, that implies the absurdity of illness, of old age, and of death. There is, he says, disagreement about the difference between man and other animals, but

> there is another very specific property that distinguishes between them and about which there can be no argument, namely the faculty of perfecting oneself; a faculty which, with the aid of circumstances, successively develops all the others, and resides in us in the species as well as in the individual, whereas the animal is at the end of several months what it will be for the rest of its life and its species is after a thousand years what it was in the first year of those thousand. Why is man alone liable to become an imbecile? Is it not that he thus returns to his primitive state and that, whereas the Beast, which has acquired nothing and also has nothing to lose, always keeps its instinct, man, losing through old age or other accidents all that his *perfectibility* had made him acquire, thus relapses lower than the Beast itself?[5]

One could not put better, or more concisely, the tragic aspect of modernity. What are we to make of decline if humanity's vocation is progress? If a human being is defined by his freedom, understood as a faculty that allows him to emancipate himself from the laws of his animal nature, to uproot himself from all the strict codes of instinct in order to advance ceaselessly toward greater cultural and moral perfection, is not his highest greatness also his surest loss? Doomed to historicity, how may he grant the slightest meaning to the inevitable dereliction that is also his lot in life? When the future takes the place of the past, when it is no longer a question of following ancient customs but of constructing a new man, old age is no longer wisdom but becomes decay. Whence, when the time comes, the frenzy of modern people to hide it. A meaningless mask, a laughable cosmetic face, which no one can completely avoid in a universe where the horizon of the future drains the field of meanings and values, where the celebration of youth, as alone promising, implies like the obverse of a medal the emptiness of old age that one had better try to hide.

Will cosmetic surgery replace religion? It is not certain, on this point at least, that the struggle goes in our favor, any more than that we are really capable of escaping a dilemma often most correctly rendered in caricature. Enlightenment philosophers tried it, and all our progressive thinkers following them, with Marx at their head, are aware that their ideal runs into the difficulty Rousseau caught sight of. They have offered us the following consolation: Yes, the individual deteriorates, but his total decline, which is senseless at his level of particularity, nonetheless is meaningful at the level of the species. In this way each thinker adds his contribution, however modest, to the edifice of science. "Great individuals" even rise, for this secular model, to a kind of immortality in that they get consigned to our new sacred texts, our history books. This is how scientism, for the nineteenth century, could so easily become the secular equivalent of now dead religions.

Yet this change is quite fragile: How, in a world where the individual finally comes into his own, in a society based on human rights, where autonomy stands opposed to every form of communitarianism, does one satisfy himself with what holds only for an anonymous, abstract entity, "the species"? What is essential, they say, is to participate, to add one's bit. Well, yes. But is not this essential something merely accessory, a pathetic joke as regards the individual who leaves the world, disappearing forever? Kierkegaard, concealing his work behind pseudonyms, tried to avoid these celebrations. The religion of progress, of the secular immortality of a name engraved for eternity on "universal history," of the work passed on to posterity, all this was merely ersatz. The ultimate reality, the only one that matters when the question is the meaning of existence, is not the "exemplary," but rather the unique individual, one with no equivalent. With the rise of individualism, the feeling faded that the meaning of life might come from a "contribution" added to some grandiose edifice, be it science, socialism, or the nation, not to speak of our construction of "Europe."

Thus, beneath the apparent banality of evil a real challenge confronts us. The forms of life we choose or that we submit to depend on the answers we bring, the way we come to terms with the fears they inspire. For thousands of years the sense of the sacred inspired every sphere of human culture, from art to politics, from mythology to ethics. This was illusory, perhaps, but lofty. Can our moral philosophies without transcendence compensate for this withdrawal of the divine? Should they? Might it be that ancient wisdom has been so thoroughly eclipsed that the most essential question of all—the meaning of life—has simply become a joke? Possibly, but not for certain. Yet is the only choice we have between the established religions and the different forms of psychotherapy? Or isn't there the courage of those who refuse them both? The religions willingly offer their services and show up, like smuggled goods, on the least occasion of mourning. The therapists sell us their good offices and teach us to act as we should, in six stages, with the help of psychotropic drugs if necessary. Is it really vain to hope to be able to respond in another way to the demand for meaning that imposes itself on us in these sacred moments? It would be worthwhile, at least, to make sure of this for ourselves rather than running away from such questions, which affect us all the more in that over the past two centuries or so our emotional life has been moving in a quite imprudent direction.

The Secularization and Forgetting of Meaning

One of the most striking features of our secularized universe is that we are always engaged in a project. Everything seems to say that we cannot live without fixing some objectives to be attained. To be sure, we are not unaware that our individual stories are in large part shaped from the outside, that they are out of our hands more than we control them, that we "fall" in love more than we "choose" to love, and that our professional successes or failures depend at least as much on our social and cultural heritage as on our personal talents. Admitting this may do homage to the social sciences, but it must not lead us to overlook a fundamental fact: even if we could in some way control our destiny—reach, so to speak, complete autonomy—we would still situate ourselves in relation to some ends. This is so in every regard: professional, cultural, educational, leisure, aesthetic, political, moral, affective, touristic. And when none are apparent, it is always easy to enter the cycle of consumption, to go shopping and to sacrifice something to this outing that so easily provides a goal for the least of our walks.

Inside these little plans, which are like bubbles closed in on themselves, our actions take on a meaning. They are both oriented in a certain direction and animated by an intention that confers on them a certain significance, in our eyes as well as others'. Yet the question that makes sense of these projects escapes us. In everyday life we are no doubt aware, at every moment or practically every moment, of what we have to do to carry out this or that "useful" task, but once we begin to think about it, the utility of this utility remains opaque or doubtful.[6] The "meaning of meaning"— the ultimate significance of all these particular meanings—is lacking. Most often this impression is fleeting and we have only to go back to our activities to get rid of it. It is to such a course that the modern citizen is constantly and everywhere summoned, under the threat of falling into that "lazy existence" already denounced by Hegel.

These few moments of indecision, however, are the sign of a very tangible fact. After the relative withdrawal of religion, after the death of the great utopian schemes that once set our actions within the horizon of a sweeping design, the question of meaning no longer finds any place where it can be collectively expressed. Formerly a matter for faith, today it is on the way to becoming null and void, not to say ridiculous. We feel this even before we understand it. The ancient question of "the meaning of existence" smacks of metaphysics. It seems reserved for a certain age of life, adolescence with its upheavals; for most adults it is to be confined to the strict limits of the private sphere. It appears publicly, and then hardly at all, only in certain exceptional circumstances, mourning or serious illness. Even then it gets funneled through the channel of banalities and polite phrases, those meant for exactly such a time.

Nonetheless, the modern citizen is frustrated. Without being drawn to the extremes of religious or mystical motifs (as secularism requires), he has the feeling that he is not on earth only to purchase automobiles or ever better stereo systems. Money, fame, power, seduction, of course, do seem like values to him, but relative ones. He would happily exchange them for others, thought to be more profound, such as love or friendship. It is not that the former are to be condemned, but even if we are unaware of humanity's final destination—even more so if we think the question is outdated—they don't seem able to constitute an ultimate end.

The hypothesis I want to formulate is that there is nothing anecdotal about this relative feeling of emptiness, that it is, quite to the contrary, structurally linked to one of the most essential motifs of secular existence. I say "relative" because I am aware of its fleeting aspect. One can live in our modern societies, and not too badly, without ever posing the fundamental questions I am invoking here. One can even run into material difficulties there that lead, at least for a time, to our setting such questions aside. Some will judge them to be pathetic and useless, others will see in them only an intellectual luxury. For the former, Hegel's statement that "once one has found a wife and a career, one is done with the questions life poses" will suffice. For the latter, the right political project will get us going again and put a happy end to an uneasiness whose metaphysical appearance reflects the lack of any concrete solutions.

Nonetheless, I persist in thinking that the idea, so often advanced, of a momentary void that a new "plan" can immediately fill is superficial. To say that Marxism was a religion of earthly salvation is no doubt not incorrect. And it is true that utopian schemes have, over the decades, given meaning to individual lives—both to those who believed in them and to those who fought against them, because they fought against them. Everyone in this sense can have his objectives and situate his action in some meaningful frame. What is more, we can clearly see how the different versions of communism could make sense only thanks to a genuine religious structure, one that today has disappeared. Even in their most secularized materialist versions they implied the idea of a "beyond" to present existence. Moreover, they conceived of this beyond in a theological way, both as superior to individuals and as inscribed in a salvific moment, that of the revolution—a secular equivalent of conversion. They conferred an overall significance on the militant project of self-sacrifice in the name of a cause that, for all its being said to be material, was no less transcendent.

Despite an atheism in principle, Marxism knew how to articulate this absolute transcendence of an ideal in terms of the intimacy or radical immanence of the here and now. The militant worked for the future, for future generations, for the advent of a perfect society, a paradise on earth, but this aspiration for a beyond was incarnated in a series of concrete practices that claimed to give meaning to the least details of earthly life. Conversely, the most modest of everyday tasks, selling newspapers at a factory gate or organizing a meeting, were rooted in the immaterial horizon of a better world. Religion, *religere*, to bind, one often says, following an etymology that, however contested, is nonetheless eloquent: it was this connection of the here and elsewhere that ensured the bond among militants. Reading the newspaper was their morning prayer. There, whatever might have occurred, they could detect that famous "meaning of history" in which their personal existence, however modest, played some small part.

In large part, the extraordinary power of fascination that communism exercised for a century and a half lay in this secular reworking of religion.[7] How else are we to make sense of the fact that dozens, even hundreds of millions of people threw themselves wholeheartedly into it? Religion is irreplaceable as a source of meaning. And God knows that after the two world wars meaning was needed. To the point that after the Second World War Marxism finally seemed to be the only large-scale doctrine capable of inscribing the reality of meaninglessness onto an optimistic vision of history and of facing up to two new incarnations of the devil: Nazism and colonial imperialism. In retrospect, it is difficult to see how an intellectual could have preserved any confidence in the values of liberal democracy and European "civilization" in 1945!

I say this not to legitimate, but to try to understand the scale of the illusion—and of the disillusion that was to follow.

It is this relation to meaning, in world history as well as in personal life, that has vanished with nothing having come along to take its place. And it was owing to the secularization of our universe that a doctrine that was still slightly religious was going to collapse in the West even before *perestroika* would put an end to the Soviet camp. This is why the end of communism implies an even deeper void than people have said, a void that cannot be filled by some substitute ideology, at least not by one lacking the same theological virtues. But here is where the shoe pinches. The growth of secularism, parallel to that of individualism, is an obstacle to any return of dogma and arguments from authority. With the collapse of Marxism, it is not just the political ideas that enlivened the life of millions of individuals that have been invalidated, but a whole theological vision of politics. We are not just crossing an empty space, some provisional return to the private sphere, soon to be replaced by the emergence of some new grand design, ecological or whatever. No, clearly the crisis is structural, "historial" if one wishes; that is, linked to the erosion that the secular and democratic universe imposes, without exception, on every form of traditional religiousness.

This also accounts for why, within the sphere of philosophy itself, the question of the meaning of life could have disappeared, to the point that simply to recall it seems old-fashioned. A strange kind of eclipse, to be sure, if we remember that over the millennia this question was at the heart of the discipline that sought (Need we remind ourselves?) to lead men to "wisdom." Contemporary thought has become scientific. But scientists describe the world for us *as it is, not as it ought to be.* No wisdom follows naturally from their labors. What is more, they hardly claim it does, concerned as they are to establish facts and truths, not to preach an ideology or an ethics, and still less to come up with some prophetic vision of the world. The failure of Marxism, which was the last attempt of this style, has vaccinated us against such ventures. In French high schools and universities, philosophy has been reduced to a meditation on other branches of knowledge or, more simply, to the teaching of its own history. One presents to the students the great doctrines of the past, "from Plato to Freud." Sometimes one invites them to "reflect," to "think for themselves," using the works of the tradition as a kind of trampoline for their own flights of fancy. All of that conforms with democratic individualism and its requirement of autonomy. Yet in this exercise, at best, each student forms only a few subjective opinions. One acquires, in the best of cases, a bit of learning, a few intellectual catchwords, and maybe a minimum of elementary moral convictions, most often marked by the ideology of human rights. This is useful baggage, no doubt, but singularly insufficient with regard to the ideal inscribed within the word "philosophy": love of wisdom. This love develops in an uncontrolled way, at the margin of academic disciplines. It seeks to find its way among the resurgence of ancient forms of spirituality, reformulated for today's taste and retranslated into today's language. So it has been for twenty years now, starting with the rediscovery of Buddhism in the West. But this quest for meaning, taken in terms of the logic of democratic secularization, often ends in an even greater blindness.

Buddhism Revisited: From the Forgetfulness of Meaning to Its Negation

The sixties: California, in revolt against a Western civilization it judges to be decadent and repressive, rediscovers the Orient. Works by Alan Watts and Daisets Susuki on Zen Buddhism are all the rage. It is not from the plateaus of Tibet or the waters of the Ganges that Buddhism comes to us, but from the Pacific coast. And as always, Europe as a whole falls in behind America. The best-known rock stars present themselves before the most prestigious gurus, and the voyage to Katmandu becomes the obligatory passage of a new rite of initiation. Far from being outmoded, this fashion continues to grow today, which is surprising given that the revolts fell silent and the countercultural utopias have also died. There are no end of books that propose to tell us how to live, that invite us to discover "the Way," that promise to initiate us into Eastern spirituality, to rediscover the virtues of natural medicines. Is this foolish, sectarian? A kind of dangerous irrationalism for the principles of democracy?

Early acquaintance with the texts of Greek antiquity convinced me it is an error to want to read great works at second hand, to address our questions to them naively, when the depths of history separate us from them in an irremediable way. What can we understand, from San Francisco or Paris, of Eastern religions known only through approximate translations, with no regard for historical and cultural distances? Yet if this phenomenon attains such a scale among us, it must somehow say something to us, must fill some void—starting, of course, with the one that leaves in eclipse the question of meaning. It does so, however, in a very odd way, even contributing, it seems to me, to its own eradication.

What, in effect, is the essential message that most Westerners first get from Buddhism? André Comte-Sponville, who can be seen reflecting this in his first books, put it concisely: in encountering a received idea, it is not hope (*espoir*) but, in the proper sense of the term, despair (*dés-espoir*) that is the condition of genuine happiness. To be persuaded of this, we need only reflect a moment. To hope, by definition, is to be not happy but expectant, lacking, desiring in an unsatisfied, impotent manner: "To hope is to desire without enjoying, without knowing, without being able."[8] Without enjoying, since one never hopes except for what one does not have; without knowing, since hope always implies a certain amount of ignorance as regards the realization of the ends one is seeking; without being able, it being given that no one would hope for something whose realization seems obvious. Not only does hope set up a negative tension in us, it also makes us lose the present. Preoccupied by a better future, we forget that the only life worth living—the only one, simply, there is—is the one that unfolds before our eyes here and now. As a Tibetan proverb puts it, the present moment and the person facing me always count more than anything else.

Why in these conditions "turn to hope"? Better instead to flee it like a kind of hell, if one believes this Hindu aphorism from the fifteen century: "The despairing person is happy. . . . For hope is the greatest form of suffering and despair the greatest blessing."[9] Wise is the person who knows how to let go of the world and attain a state of "nonattachment." If any hope does remain, it is that of one day reaching, through patience and exercise, the beatitude of despair.

Therefore it is through reflection on death and evil in all its forms that we have to situate the meaning of this life. Listen to the Dalai Lama: "In reflecting on death and impermanence, you will begin to give meaning to your life,"[10] for only such meditation, if done right, can aid us to let go of all those "attachments"[11] that render us vulnerable to suffering, whether these attachments are of a material or an emotional order:[12] "Whoever practices the dharma [the Buddha's teaching] thinks daily about death, reflects on human suffering—the torments of birth, of aging, of sickness and death. It is like dying mentally each day. Because of his familiarity with it, he will be ready when he ends up encountering it."[13] Beyond the beneficial effect produced by this preparation, the numerous and difficult exercises and practices it implies will also offer the beneficial effect of assigning a clear goal to human existence as a whole. "The advantage of being conscious of death is to give a meaning to life, and to taste its approach means that one dies without regret."[14] The Dalai Lama insists on this point: "In reflecting on death and in being constantly conscious of it, your life takes on its full meaning."[15]

The aim of an authentic existence? It lies in the radical deconstruction of the illusions of the ego. This is what, always, is "attached." This is what, always, egoistically, resists and clings to its different possessions instead of blending, as though in anticipation, into the universal, impersonal spirit to which it ought wisely to learn to belong. For the illusion of attachment, the one that makes us "strongly desire beautiful people, beautiful things, and pleasant experiences,"[16] is only a consequence of the initial illusion on which all others depend: that of the "self."[17] Hence "the antidote that will eliminate these illusions is the wisdom that realizes the absence of any self."[18]

Here we can see the abyss that separates Buddhist reincarnation from Christian resurrection. The error would be to imagine that the former is the "Oriental" analogue of the immortality of a personal soul. It is its exact opposite. Not a reward for faithfulness to the divine, but the punishment reserved for one who has not yet attained genuine awakening, for one for whom a lifetime was not enough to free himself from the illusions of the ego, and who thus sees himself condemned to return again to that vast ocean of suffering that is life as a prisoner of the cycles of birth and death (samsara). In other words, another chance for the personal ego, which is wholly bad, finally to abolish itself to the profit of the mind-spirit that is wholly impersonal. For the Oriental masters, "the subject is not what is to be saved, but rather that from which one must save oneself."[19] In encountering this idea that the gulf between East and West is insurmountable and that the two cultures are permanently impervious to each other, we may also rediscover in our philosophical tradition some equivalents of this praise of despair.[20] Among the Stoics, of course, but also in Spinoza's definition of freedom as "the comprehension of necessity" or again in Nietzsche, when he pleads for the "innocence of becoming," for that grace of the artist who creates with neither "bad conscience" nor "*ressentiment.*"

Their ethics of despair is attractive. Undoubtedly it brings precious comfort to those who dream of being done once and for all with the anxieties of finitude. Who would not like living in grace, being able to live at each moment without reticence or prevarication, a life in the present where, indeed, questions about the future or nostalgia for the past risk spoiling it for those who live in the dimension of a "project"? Yet a suspicion creeps in. It is sometimes said of the God of Christians that he is too good to be true, that there are, in short, so many reasons to invent him that he must actually be an invention. For myself, I am more inclined to think this of a wisdom too forgetful of the self to be completely honest.[21] Here, quite simply, is why.

I have tried, but I am unable to find the universe so perfect, or the cosmic order so harmonious, that the requirement to adhere to it without any reservations, to the point of always loving it in the present, makes any sense. This argument may seem trivial, and no doubt it is, but it still seems to me irrefutable. How can one recommend reconciliation with what is—total adhesion to destiny, *amor fati*—when the world presents us with the face of Auschwitz or Rwanda? Why such an imperative, and for whom?

For the monk, one will say, who lives on his plateaus between heaven and earth. And one will prescribe for us, no doubt, some retreat. But the monk, wherein we hear *monos*, one, lives alone. He does not marry and has neither family nor friends. Unlike Christ, he doesn't know human love. He wants to eradicate his ego. So be it. But we do not, or even worse, we resolutely want the opposite. Some diet plans propose to let us eat and still get thin. In this same sense we want to love and not suffer, to take what our individualistic universe offers as the best and correct it with a few doses of Buddhism. But this won't work, and as for Buddhism, for anyone who is not a monk—anyone, therefore, who doesn't take it seriously—can it ever be anything more than a spiritual diet?[22]

Let us even allow for the monk's life. He still is, in a way, an ego. But how may an ego deconstruct the illusions of the ego? If he *wants* despair, is he not in a way still caught up in hope, and if he *seeks* to emancipate himself from every project, is he not still caught in a project? A performative contradiction. The dogmatic thinker is a thinker; he has just forgotten to think through his own thinking. The "sage" is always outside himself, always discerns what "must be," falling back into the critique of the present, wanting to change the world if only by inviting his disciples to practice detachment. There is a paradox, in which we can see the great depth of Buddhism or its Achilles' heel: as the meaning of our life it assigns attaining a vision of the world in which the question of meaning disappears.

The Personal Structure of Meaning

The point is worth reflecting on. What, indeed, does the word "meaning" mean? Let us begin from an experience we all share, precisely that of looking for the meaning of a word one does not know, a word, for example, in a foreign language. Oddly, the formula that comes to mind is, "Now what could that *mean?*" [In French this is, literally, "want to say" (*veut dire*)—Trans.] This is a curious way of putting things, for if such is the case, it is difficult to see a priori what the *will* is doing here. Why not just be content to ask, "What does this word say?" Isn't this question sufficient to obtain the wished-for information? Why "wanting," which in this case entails the *intention of a subject?* Is the underlying presence of a *person,* an *ego,* so essentially tied to the very idea of meaning that we cannot do without it in even such a banal question?

The answer is obvious. For a word to possess a meaning it has to be a sign with a double exteriority or, if you will, a double transcendence: on the one hand, the transcendence of what is signified (or of a referent—the difference is not important here); on the other, that of the intention of a subject, necessarily assumed in the background.

Let us consider an example. If a road sign has a "meaning," it is not just because it points in some direction (something, for example, stars also do, which are beautiful but denuded of meaning) but because it was "intentionally" created by someone (even "someone" anonymous, like a highway engineer) who wants to communicate with us and transmit certain information.

One can posit the following axiom: Anything that is not the effect of a will, even when unconscious, like a slip of the tongue, anything that is not in some way the manifestation of a subjectivity, has no meaning, makes no sense. Thus, for example, no one asks the "meaning" of a tree, a table, a dog. Yet one can ask the meaning of a word, a remark, an attitude, a facial expression, a work of art, or any other sign in general that we assume, rightly or wrongly, is the expression of some willing, the sign of some personality. What does it *mean* to say? Here is why asking for the meaning of a star, a tree, or an animal would be a sign of superstition. To do so would be to consider, like Berkeley, that nature is the language of a hidden will, that of God. Here also is why asking the question of the meaning of evil is possible only from a perspective where one assumes the reality of a free subject, of a responsible will that is the source of this question.

Only humanism, then, turns out to be capable of responding to the question of meaning, while all the forms of antihumanism invite us to abolish it in favor of a surrender to being or life. For meaning exists only in a relation of one person to another, in the bond that unites two wills, whether or not we think of them as purely human. Those cosmologies that call on us to sublimate the ego, to elevate ourselves above the illusions of subjectivity in order to free ourselves from ourselves and prepare ourselves for death,

all assign a single meaning to human life—to act in such a way
that once and for all one gets rid of the problem of meaning.

And this is why, furthermore, they are comforting, why they fit
so well with contemporary materialism, since they cover over the
fundamental paradox of our situation. As humanists we can never
do away completely with the question of meaning, even when the
universe of work and consumption that surrounds us pushes us
from every direction to do so. We do not stop wanting to unravel
the significance of what happens to us, and when something bad
occurs, when death strikes, with its absurdity, we cannot hold back
the question Why? Yet as disillusioned, even secular humanists, we
cannot answer, for we no longer possess that absolute, properly
divine subject who once came to put an end to the infinite series
of questions and partial meanings. It is this contradiction that constitutes, in the deepest sense, the setting of the question of meaning
in democratic societies. This is what today's new forms of spirituality want to annul by persuading us that it is enough to love fate,
even though there is nothing lovable about it. It is as though, after
the "death of God," even the slightest sense of transcendence has
to disappear. Yet it may be that instead of fleeing this contradiction, we need to deepen it and to think it through. It may be that
not all transcendence has disappeared to the profit of some cosmic
order or the individual as king, that instead it has been transformed to adjust to the limits that modern humanism henceforth
imposes on it.

The End of Theological Ethics

Ever since Nietzsche, or even beginning with the philosophers of
the Enlightenment and their critique of superstition, any number
of analyses have considered the birth of the democratic universe
as the effect of a break with religion. "The death of God," the
"disenchantment of the world" (Weber, Gauchet), the end of the
"theological-political" (Carl Schmitt), "secularization"—as vague
and as controversial as they may be, these expressions today sym-
bolize different interpretations of the same reality: the advent of a
secular universe within which belief in the existence of God no

longer structures our political space.[23] It is not that such a belief, as Gauchet emphasizes, has disappeared. Rather, it has become, for the majority among us, a personal affair, something for the private sphere—the public sphere being taken as assuming a strict neutrality in this regard.

For most of us, therefore, the moral law, like juridical law, has lost its sacred character, or at least its tie to revealed religious sources. Like everything else in the modern culture it participates in, it is "on a human scale." The end of theological ethics—that eclipse of moral theology that Jean Paul II continues to denounce—thus puts us into a circle from which it is difficult, even impossible, to extract ourselves. Existential questions whose answers went more or less without saying in the traditional universe rise up with an unexpected sharpness in democratic societies, where they are caught up in the infinite maelstrom of autonomy. Marriage, children's education, fidelity, one's relation to money, to one's body—all the questions raised by the evolution of science and technology—are no longer governed by easily identifiable rules. In truth, the more these questions arise, the less easy it is to respond to them in a collective way, stripped as we are a priori of any established criterion. And owing to this very fact, the more these criteria fade along with the fading of the world of tradition and of moral theology, the more numerous are the aspects of life that fall into the range of questions for the individual.

So we have ethics as grounded on man. But does the advent of modern humanism then signify that we have done once and for all with every form of spirituality? For most of us, atheists or agnostics, partisans of a strict secularism, the obligatory answer is yes. It is taken for granted that the great secular ethical theories born during the eighteenth century, if reactualized and applied to our questions today, *suffice*. Kantian republicanism, for example, has been prolonged by the concern to perfect an "ethics of discussion" (Habermas), to integrate a "principle of responsibility" (Jonas, Apel), and English utilitarianism can now call on mathematical models in its "calculation of pleasures and pains." But at bottom it is the great moral visions of the world that still underlie our judicial systems. In thinking of the ancients, or even today's believers, we spontaneously tend to situate their values among the inevitable "survivals" of outdated traditions. We say to ourselves something like this: "They had religion (or cosmology), we have ethics." And that, in effect, suffices for us to know how to lead our day-to-day lives. There is no need of religion in order to be honest or charitable. No need to believe in God in order to do our "duty." Even more, the struggle for secularism is, rightly, a priority. And in the case of Islam, it rightly takes place through the critique of a theology that seems incapable of thinking of its own separation from the political realm. Our republican, not to say anticlerical, feeling is enough to keep us alert to the possible effects of a "religious edict." The name Salman Rushdie will suffice to remind us of this fact.

The cause is well understood, but it is not in question here. What is, is the claim of any secular ethical theory having come to maturity to have done away with the question of transcendence. In at least two ways it seems to me they are incapable of doing so.

It is clear, in the first place, that the requirement of "concern for the other" and even, should the need arise, for "giving of one-self" have not disappeared from the leading theories of secular ethics. Whether they prescribe a struggle against egoism in the name of disinterested action or prefer the happiness of the greatest number over that of any one person, our modern moral philosophies put forth ideals that in some way are meant to be *superior to life*. Here, in a way that already upset Nietzsche, is the most certain criterion of a kind of thought that is still "religious." To suppose that some values transcend life itself is in effect to lead us back to the most essential structure of any theology, even if it is on atheistic grounds: the difference between a "here below" and an "above and beyond." Humanist moralities do not really regret this dualism. Is it better to be red than dead, a collaborator in a concentration camp, a pacifist in the wake of Munich than to accept a just war? These questions, and others of the same order, continue to haunt the modern conscience. That cowardliness often carries the day in our personal or political behavior does not change things. These questions continue to trace out for us, even without our having to reflect on them, the boundary between good and evil. And if our commitment finds itself challenged in a more embodied, less formal way because the life of those close to us is at risk, we can see how the idea of the risk of death is far from having disappeared from the field of our moral preoccupations—as it should have, strictly speaking, if, as Nietzsche wanted, humanism had carried through the consequences of a rigorous deconstruction of religion to their ultimate end. If it had identified itself with an apology for vital forces, with an individualistic anthropology of only the "care of the self."

To this strange persistence of transcendence, of an apparently undiscoverable beyond, gets added the presentiment that even the most perfect moral philosophy is in truth not sufficient. If it is a matter above all else of "acting right," of choosing "good" rules of behavior, of applying them correctly to specific cases—and of respecting them—nothing prevents us from imagining that utilitarian or Kantian programs ought to be able to tell us without error what decisions impose themselves in each case. There should not even be any room of chance, when modern theories of justice can today make ever greater use of logical-mathematical reflection about "rational choices."[24] Indeed, logically, anybody who accepts the universalistic principles of modern ethics is well aware that the number of decisions they impose on him is not infinite and that they are in no way arbitrary. Everything is as it should be. It is impossible, for example, to be a partisan of human rights and a racist at the same time. Similarly, it is impossible from this point of view to accept a difference in status between men and women, or to consider that one's own interest comes a priori before that of others, and so forth.

We should therefore be able to conceive of a moral automaton, a robot who, given any hypothesis, does what it should do.[25] Yet it is also clear that it is not with such a creature that we would choose to pass our lives. And this is so (along with other examples) for good reason: the respect for rules, however valuable it may be, does not possess as such any *human character*, hence any *meaning*, if we admit that "to mean" [*vouloir dire*] (as we hear in the expression "What does that mean to say?") is something that belongs to a *subject*. Moral philosophy is useful and even necessary, but it remains within the negative order of the prohibition. If secular ethics, even the most sophisticated and perfect ones, are to constitute the ultimate horizon of our existence, we still will lack something, in truth something essential. And this something, of course, is the experience of those values that communtarians call "embodied" or "substantial," which in the best of cases experience makes known to us.[26] To begin with the highest among these: love (both of individuals and of those communities we belong to).

Respect for democratic forms and procedures founds the state based on the rule of law. Without a doubt it constitutes, within the moral and political order, the highest value, the indispensable fire wall. But if we were to stop there, with a formal morality and the law—and all modern moral thought comes down to this—politics itself would hardly be worth a minute of our time. This is without doubt what Camus meant when he stated that he preferred his mother to justice. It is what André Comte-Sponville develops in his *Petit traité des grandes vertus,* rejoining in this way a long tradition of which we are all well aware: if we only had love, we would have nothing to do but be moral! Presuming, of course, that it was genuine love, something that has yet to be shown, it would render superfluous every categorical imperative, every kind of incitement to respect the other, every prohibition with regard to egoism, every injunction about forgetting oneself. After all, there is generally no need to tell a mother to feed her child.

Here again it is a question of a kind of transcendence, but no longer that of a God who imposes himself on us from the outside. It is not even that of formal values, which already appear to us in some enigmatic way to surpass egoistic immanence, but rather of a transcendence that is situated beyond good and evil because it belongs to the order of meaning and not to that of mere respect for the law.

We must therefore set aside the misunderstanding according to which modernity—reduced to a "metaphysics of subjectivity"— would lie in the equation: omnipotence of the ego = narcissistic individualism = end of spirituality and of transcendence to the profit of total immersion in an anthropocentric and materialistic world of technology.

It may well be that, in exact contrast to these clichés of antimodern ideologies, humanism, far from abolishing spirituality, even to the benefit of ethics, on the contrary gives us access for the first time in history to a genuine spirituality, freed of its faded theological trappings and rooted in human beings, not in some dogmatic representative of the divine. What is new in humanism is not the values it promotes. There was no need to wait for Kant and Bentham to learn that we should not lie, rape, betray, or systematically try to harm our neighbors. The fundamental values of modern thinkers, whatever one may say here or there, are in truth not original—or really very "modern." What is new is that they are thought through starting from human beings, not deduced from a revelation that precedes and encompasses them. What is new, without a doubt, is that the indefinable transcendence they carry itself bears witness to the very core of humanity's being and that it can therefore agree with the principle of principles constituting modern humanism: the one that rejects arguments from authority.

Refusal of Arguments from Authority or Rejection of Transcendence?

The idea that they ought to accept an opinion because it is offered by some authority, whatever authority, is so essentially repugnant to modern thinkers that it can define them as such. Of course sometimes we do put our confidence in a person or an institution, but this very gesture has lost its traditional meaning. If I accept something following the judgment of others, it is in principle because I have built up "good" reasons for doing so, not because this authority imposes itself on me from the outside without any prior recognition stemming from my innermost and, if possible, considered convictions.

Some may object that reality is far from corresponding to such a principle, that individuals still follow fashions or "leaders," and that they are right to do so. Still it remains true that it is on this new conception of legitimacy rooted in the conscience of each person, not in some inherited tradition or charismatic fascination, that our democratic universe rests, as much on the political level as on the intellectual or scientific level. And it is exactly in the name of such a legitimacy that any alienation in the name of some *Führer* is ceaselessly denounced by those who claim to be representative of its ideals.

The *Meditations* of Descartes consecrated this inaugural gesture in philosophy long before it was repeated in fact by the French Revolution, a century and a half later. If we must make a clean sweep of the past and submit to the most rigorous doubt all those opinions, beliefs, and prejudices that have not passed the test of critical examination, it is because we ought not to admit among our beliefs anything other than what we can ourselves be certain of. Whence the new nature, grounded in individual conscience and not in tradition, of the unique form of certitude that comes before all others: that of a subject in relation to himself. It may well be that my opinions are false, it may well be that a deceitful God or an evil demon is amusing himself by deceiving me about everything. One thing, at least, is certain: if he is to deceive me, I must exist. The model of truth therefore lies in the absolute certitude of one's presence to oneself.

Believers sometimes describe the modern world as one where lived experience has been banished or devalued to the profit of that cold reason that triumphs in the materialistic spheres of science and commercial production. However, the rationalist principle that rejects any argument from authority is inseparable from a thoroughgoing sacralization of lived experience. It is just because religion claims to impose itself on me under the form of some external authority, a "revealed" text or clerical office—that is, in a way that seems opposed to the text of my own conscience—that it has to be submitted to the test of criticism. This, as is well known, was the fate reserved for religion by most of the philosophers of the eighteenth century, who in this way were faithful to Cartesian freedom of thought.

Therefore it is superficial to oppose "rich, tangible" experience to "overly intellectual, arid" scientific experimentation or logical argument. From the modern perspective of rejecting arguments from authority, every sphere where a belief may take shape is to be submitted to the principle of self-presence, be it spiritual, ethical, aesthetic, or even scientific. Did I really see what I believe I saw, might I be fooling myself, have I denied my senses or appealed to some other illusory artifice that may have escaped me? In such a case, the experience I believe I had will not really be *mine*, since without being aware of it I will have been literally outside myself, beside myself. Have I really thought through the sequence of reasoning that led me to admit this conclusion? If there is any question begging, any fault in my logic, there will be something like a leap, an external gap between me and my conclusion, which therefore will not really be *mine*. Have I carried out well the experiment I sought to do, correctly "isolated the variables," properly formulated my hypothesis? Otherwise the conclusions will again get away from me and I will end up in the clouds of error rather than the heaven of scientific truth. This is the kind of questioning by which that work of reasoning some call cold and detached is constantly related back to a concrete and passionate subjectivity.

Do we have here the overweening pride of the modern *ego*, which wants to make everything part of itself, to annul all dependence on an exterior (on which, however, it seems quite evident it is totally dependent)? Is it not born on earth and not from itself? Is it not plunged from birth into a language, a culture, a social and family milieu to which it belongs more than these belong to it? And does not this inaugural finitude discover within itself its inevitable mortal destiny, whereby it can master neither the place nor the hour of its own disappearance? There is an ambiguity to these questions that opposes the partisans of romanticism and those of the Enlightenment. There is no antinomy between the modern claim for autonomy and the persistence of some forms of heteronomy, even of radical dependence. On the contrary, the modern principle implies the emergence of hitherto unheard-of forms of heteronomy. It is just that this heteronomy has been rearranged, since it has to be articulated along with the new demands of the individual.

Let us not confuse the ideal of autonomy with the absurd metaphysical affirmation of the self-sufficiency of an absolute ego. To do so is simply an error. Self-presence and self-mastery, understood as antiauthoritarian principles, do not entail that every link to exteriority be annulled or challenged. Cartesian doubt itself, which is directed against inherited prejudices, does not imply that every tradition has, as such, to be rejected. Instead it requires that tradition *become mine in some way* and that, for this to happen, I put it to the test. We might say, in what is still an approximation, that in this way transcendence moves from the order of being *before* my conscience to being *after* it. There may be radical dependence, absolute transcendence, but only as first and necessarily anchored in

my own certainty and real experience, in my self-independence
and my immanence to myself.

Let us go still further. The modern principle of the refusal of
arguments from authority so little annuls dependence on alterity
that it even affirms it more than any other alternative. The question of the status of meaning, of spirituality in a secular world, is
at issue here. How, to use the language of phenomenology, are we
to think through this "transcendence in self-immanence"?

Transcendence in Immanence

In *The Idea of Phenomenology*, Husserl assigns to "rigorous science,"
which he means to found, the task of removing a classical contradiction in modern philosophy that goes back to Descartes. On the
one hand, from the point of view of a subject who can be absolutely certain only of the immediately given data of its consciousness, the relation to the world is not self-evident. Recall the old
argument about dreaming, which makes us believe in the existence
of objects that have no reality beyond our awareness of them.
Therefore all "transcendence" is problematic.[27] Whence the temptation of an idealism that denies the existence of the material world
and reduces being to representation. Yet I cannot completely ex-
trapolate from the fact that the contents of my consciousness are
related, even within my innermost consciousness, to objects that
do indeed seem external to me.[28] When I open my eyes to the
world, it appears to me in an indisputable way to be something I
did not create out of my own consciousness. I therefore have in me
(immanence), the constraining sense of something "outside me"
(transcendence).

At first sight the problem seems almost scholastic. But in light
of this apparently "technical" question, phenomenology develops
a thesis whose import goes well beyond the narrow framework of
a philosophy professor. It seeks to demonstrate that the contents of
my consciousness, in a paradox that is really what is at issue, *contain
more than they actually contain*, that there is, so to speak, something
invisible in everything that is visible, an absence at the heart of all
presence. Without having to think about it, I always "perceive"
certain structures that are not, in the true sense, effectively given

in my awareness, as though this latter were a purely objective mirror, a simple apparatus for registering things (like a camera or a tape recorder). To cite one well-known example, when I say that I "see" a cube, in fact I only ever perceive three faces of it. "Effectively immanent" in me in the strict sense are these three faces, not the cube itself, whose six faces cannot be seen "all at once" and therefore transcend what is actually given in my subjective representation. And yet this transcendence is in fact, in another sense, also "in me." I need no demonstration to "know" that I am looking at a cube. No one says, "I see three squares, and I deduce from this that I must affirm that it is a cube." So it is not false to affirm that my perception contains "more than it contains."[29] Another example: When I hear a musical passage, it does not reduce to a series of isolated notes with no connection between them (actual immanence). On the contrary, it constitutes—and in an immediate way, apart from any rational operation—a certain structure that transcends this actual immanence, without being imposed on me from the outside like an argument from authority.

This "immanent transcendence" contains within itself, par excellence, the ultimate significance of lived experiences. The musical passage would have no meaning if I perceived it only as a string of notes separated from one another like atoms (as I would if I were simply a tape recorder). It therefore must be possible to think about and to describe transcendence without leaving the sphere of immanence. Without being a demonstration, or possessing the exactitude of the mathematical and physical sciences, phenomenology will be no less a "rigorous" science in its description of the objective constraints imposed on us. One can see that such an undertaking will be highly complex, but also highly diverse, since the "excess" characterizing those forms of transcendence situated, so to speak, "in us" can belong to every intellectual domain, from aesthetics to science, in passing through ethics or religion.

Without getting ahead of ourselves as regards the particularity of such labor, we can already understand how it may respond to the demands of a modern reflection on transcendence. This latter is given, apart from any argument from authority, in the immanence of subjective lived experience and therefore *starting from it*, so to speak, as its "downstream" side, not as something imposed on it from "upstream." This further suggests that revelation, if there is any revelation,[30] has to be reinterpreted from this perspective of a new, nontraditional relation to the individual. Concerning God, the phenomenologist will not tell us that he commands us, in the name of some imposed tradition, to follow this or that law, to attain this or that end, but rather will say that he "comes to us in the idea" and does this through the face of our neighbor, of the other human person.[31] According to the profound insight of Rousseau and Fichte, the human face is immediately, before any reasoning on our part, apart from any demonstration, the bearer of a meaning that surpasses me and summons me.[32] And it is from this summons, which demands a response, a responsibility, that ethics emerges. A phenomenology of transcendence may thus delineate the space for a "secular spirituality." It is by starting from the human as such and its own core that a certain idea of the sacred unveils itself.

We must therefore attempt to circumscribe the factual reality of those forms of "dependence" or transcendence that the modern principle of the refusal of arguments of authority does not forbid us to recognize, but on the contrary invites us to think about in new ways.

The Weight of the Past, the Birth of Historical Consciousness, and the Discovery of the Unconscious

Sociology, psychoanalysis, history, all constantly come back to this. It is even their real object: we are all, in whatever way one may wish, "heirs." And those who yield to the individualist illusions of the tabula rasa, from hyperbolic Cartesians to French revolutionaries who claimed to be able to rebuild the political world starting again from year I, pay the highest price for this return of the repressed. But it would be an error to believe, as traditionalists do, that the metaphysical illusions of a self-founding subject really go with the modern principle. Instead, they contradict it. Modernity lies not in refusing the weight of historicity but instead in thinking about this historicity in a new way, no longer that of an imposed tradition, but rather that of a reason that brings itself to conclude that outside itself the irrational necessarily exists.

Let us pause for a moment to consider this assertion. The principle of reason affirms more radically than ever the dependence of human beings on what precedes, surrounds, and succeeds them. "Everything happens for a reason." This formula could be understood, albeit wrongly, as saying that everything is rational and therefore that the subject who commits himself to scientific inquiry will be able to bring the world under his control, to incorporate it so to speak into logic, through a process of domination in which traditionalists see the most dangerous aspect of modernity. Yet this same principle can also be read, more correctly, in a wholly different way. It then says that my life will always outrun me, that the order of reasons that binds me to the past is infinite, as much in the collective order (of history and sociology) as in the individual one (of psychoanalysis). Yes, I may try to overcome this dependence as much as possible, but I also have to accept its interminable character, the impossibility of bringing this will to self-mastery to a final conclusion. Whence the feeling that the task of the sciences, contrary to what antiquity thought, will never be completed. As Kant had already seen, the principle of reason turns into its opposite: in affirming the indefinite character of the series of causes and effects, it invites us to accept the idea that any "end of the chain" will always escape us and that it is, for just this reason, rational to presuppose the irrational.

If no longer traditional, no longer based on revelation, our relation to the past is still in some ways heteronomous. What the principle of reason adds is not the abolition of historicity, the eradication of the past, but rather the fact that these are connected to me in a quite specific way, more as a product of my reason than as given to me from the outside. Hence I can accept my dependence, I can acknowledge a transcendence of my own initiative in my immanence to myself, without which I would again give in to the easy temptation of the principle of authority. Therefore we can admit the discovery of the social and individual unconscious, but without seeing in it any reintroduction of a traditionalist principle into the heart of modernity;[33] instead we can reformulate it in terms that fit modern consciousness.

The appearance of the idea of the unconscious was not due to some mysterious fall from divine transcendence into the "self."[34] It is to be explained instead because, starting from the principle of reason, this idea becomes for the ego, even for the person who most clings to the illusion of self-sufficiency, an inevitable conclusion. The schoolboy opposition of the figures of Freud and Descartes is too simplistic. It would be better instead to distinguish two ways of thinking about the unconscious. The traditional one situates the unconscious in the immemorial past of a revelation that is supposed to lie at the origin of all history. The modern one infers it from the principle of sufficient reason. The theory of the Freudian slip provides a telling example. The missing act is above all *the effect* of a reason that escapes me. And the fact that this reason may often be unreasonable, passionate, and based on instincts ("dynamic") does not change anything as regards the fundamental rationality of the analytic approach. This is a paradox of reason, which Kant will describe so well with the antinomies that lead us to metaphysical madness. It is at once a project of self-mastery and of mastery over the world and yet an affirmation of the most radical dispossession possible, that of our unfathomable tie to the past.

To this first intellectual insight, which will be swallowed up by the social sciences, corresponds another, still more profound opening on the ethical plane.

From Here to There: Transcendence within the Limits of Humanism

Not only am I plunged from the beginning of my life into a world that I neither sought nor created, but furthermore the meaning of my birth and death escapes me. No doubt I can attempt to learn their scientific conditions, to analyze the processes of the reproduction and aging of my cells. But nothing in the biological approach, however relevant or interesting it may be, will allow me to master either the miracle of life or the conceptual significance of my finitude. Here again there is an aspect of invisibility, of exteriority, or if you prefer, of transcendence that prolongs what reason requires me to discover in the determination of the past.

Even the most developed sciences can only describe or even partially explain what is. But the sheer fact that things "are"—the "question of Being"—does not belong to them. Regarding this, they can tell us nothing, and today as yesterday, the entire mystery remains. When astrophysics speaks of a Big Bang, no doubt it intersects with the old theological, then metaphysical question of the origin of the universe, the one that Leibniz, in the seventeenth century, made the center of all philosophy: Why is there something rather than nothing? This is why, beyond its inevitable technical details, it speaks to the interest of a wider public. We sense, however, even as we hope for a solid answer at last, that it will never succeed in lifting the mysteries that surround the question of origins. One essential, structural obstacle blocks the way: to get there astrophysics would have to go beyond its field of competence, to become again in some fashion theology or metaphysics. In other words, it would have to stop being empirical—and then its expected solidity would evaporate. This obligatory renouncement gives an unexpected significance to the age-old finitude of mortals.

In the philosophy of the seventeenth century, human beings were still thought of starting from God and, if I may put it this way, "after" God. There was first of all the Creator, the absolute and infinite being, and in relation to him, human beings were defined as a lack, as finitude. Whence their well-known weaknesses, their congenital ignorance, yes, but for all that also their irrepressible propensity to sin. This perspective, in which God came logically *before* human beings, also went with a theological ethics as the religious foundation of morality.

It is this hierarchy that the appearance of the modern sciences and of a secular space abolishes. As Ernst Cassirer has suggested, during the century of the Enlightenment the primacy of human existence found itself affirmed in every domain, to the point that God began to appear as an "idea" of the humanity he was held to have created and that, in the words of Voltaire, "he then turned over to man." From Kant to Feuerbach, Marx, or Freud, this emphasis on the human intellect will be taken ever more seriously.

On the moral level, this reversal sounded the death knell of theological ethics. It is within human beings, with the reason and freedom that constitute their dignity, that the principles of respect for the other have to be grounded, not in some divinity. And in the eyes of these philosophers Christ himself, the God-Man par excellence, was already nothing more than a saintly person—an individual who realized in himself and applied to those around him the universalizing principles whose most adequate expression would soon appear in the Declaration of the Rights of Man in 1789. He is, Kant and his disciples will say, "the moral idea of humanity," something that earned them the damning accusation of being atheists. If ethics by itself turns out to be what Christianity teaches, there is no longer any need for God, or even Christ, to ground it.

This movement is well known. Yet the description of it ordinarily given avoids the crucial question: What role then remains for religion? This question is all the harder to set aside because the Enlightenment philosophers often wanted to think of themselves as Christians and because they thought, sincerely, that they were elevating the comprehension of the message of the Gospels to its most authentic level. And in fact, far from disappearing, this message continues to form the horizon of secular moralities.

Here is what, I believe, the decisive significance of this "religious revolution" comes down to: *Without disappearing, the contents of Christian theology no longer come before ethics, to ground its truth, but come after it, to give it a meaning.* Human beings therefore no longer have to appeal to God in order to understand that they should respect others, should treat them as ends and not just means. Atheism and morality can in this way be reconciled. But the reference to the divine, to that idea of a God whom Levinas, remaining faithful to the tradition of the Enlightenment, will say "comes to mind," still does not vanish. On the contrary, it exists for fundamental reasons. It comes, so to speak, to confer a meaning on the fact of respect for the law, in order to add hope to duty, love to respect, the Christian element to the Jewish.

The Hypotheses of This Book

The first hypothesis of this book is that the question of meaning and the question of the sacred—of why it may not be unreasonable to think of *sacrifice*—are inseparable. The second is that these two questions are interconnected today based on a twofold process. On the one hand, there is the "disenchantment of the world" or, to put it a better way, the broad movement of the *humanization of the divine* that since the eighteenth century has characterized the rise of secularism in Europe. In the name of a refusal of arguments from authority and of the freedom of conscience, the content of revelation has continued to become "humanized" over the past two centuries. It is against this tendency that the pope publishes his encyclicals. And it is in terms of this context that we have to interpret his struggles, whatever we may think of them. But in parallel to all this, there has also been a slow and inexorable *divinization of the human* of which we are a part, bound to the birth of modern "love," whose specificity historians of *mentalités* have recently taught us to decipher. The most contemporary problems in ethics bear witness to this: from bioethics to humanitarian action, it is human beings as such that appear as sacred today. How then does the question of the meaning of life ground itself in this era of man made god?

In attempting to trace out the contours of this question, I shall first examine the ultimate twists in the slow process of the humanization of the divine. Since the eighteenth century, "theism"—the idea of a "practical faith" that would not be the conclusion of a philosophical argument—has been affirmed ever more clearly, even in the very universe of Christianity itself. This happens starting from what is a humanist problem. "Starting from," that is, and also *after* and *according to* it, but in no way prior to it. From now on the movement goes from human beings to God, and not conversely. It is autonomy that leads to heteronomy, without this latter's coming to impose itself on an individual or contradicting such autonomy. Traditionalist Christians will see in this the supreme sign of human pride. Secular Christians, on the contrary, can see in it the advent of an authentic faith that at last is based on the eclipsing of any theological ethics.[35] Here is what is at stake in the argument reopened by Jean Paul II's encyclical *Veritatis Splendor.* It opposes the partisans of a return to moral theology and those who, on the contrary, offer "the praise of conscience"[36] to the point of, even within the church, calling for an "ethics of discussion." Transcendence is not negated by this reversal of perspective. It is in fact inscribed, as an idea, within human reason. But it is at the heart of an immanence to the self, as entailed by the rejection of any argument from authority, that it now manifests itself to a subject who claims, at least on the moral plane, an ideal of autonomy.

CHAPTER ONE

The Humanization of the Divine

FROM JOHN PAUL II TO DREWERMANN

T he church resists, and not without good motives. If the tendency toward humanization of the sources of law, morals, and culture implies calling into question the vertical forms of transcendence of an earlier day,[1] how is the credibility of a moral theology to maintain itself? How can one reconcile revelation and conscience or, to recall the terms of Jean Paul II, "the splendor of truth" and "individual liberty"? Isn't Christianity doomed to become a simple faith, a feeling of piety arising from the ground of secular moralities that will now provide it with what is essential about its concrete contents? The disenchantment of the world does not stop with the mere separation of religion and politics. It is not confined to the end of theological ethics, which is indispensable for the coming about of a secular public space; rather, it produces, in its depths, effects on individual beliefs and private opinions. Any number of inquiries confirm this. Most Catholics have become "deists," in Voltaire's sense of this term.[2] Certainly they preserve a sense of transcendence, but more and more they are abandoning traditional dogma in favor of conversion to the ideology of human rights. They still call themselves Catholics, but they submit the pope's commandments to the humanist test of critical examination, and hardly any of them believe any longer in the real immortality of the soul, the factual virginity of Mary, or even the existence of the devil.

The Humanization or Secularization of Religion Itself

In this sense, two trees conceal the forest. Two more or less conventional kinds of discourse hide the real depth of the arguments that today are found everywhere in the universe of religion.

The first of these—"God's revenge"—applies to all types of fundamentalism. It asserts, sometimes based on good arguments, that we are experiencing a "return of the religious." The Western world, however imbued with its sense of historical superiority, will secrete its own antidote—unless the reaction is found outside it in the last spasms of decolonialization, another variation of this type of discourse. Khomeini's brand of Islam, Monsignor Lefebvre's brand of Christianity, and the Judaism of the Israeli far right have to be understood as different faces of a single worrisome phenomenon: integralism.

On the other side, however, every serious sociological inquiry shows the amplitude of the movement of secularization that is winning the democratic European world. This is so to such a point that we ought to speak, especially with regard to youth, of a veritable "de-Christianization."[3]

There is something true about these analyses. But they also have the drawback of concealing the way institutionalized religions themselves react, so to speak from within themselves, to the problems posed by the secularizing of the world. From this point of view, the concepts of integralism and de-Christianization are wholly insufficient. They do not allow us to take into account the way the immense majority of believers live and conceive of their relationship to the modern world. They contribute, on the contrary, to making invisible, hence undiscussable in public space, the two crucial questions that today divide the church. Yet, as we shall see, they reveal effects produced by the emancipation of believers from traditional figurations of the theological-political. As for nonbelievers, they too show to a tendency toward the humanization of religion that merits our attention and reflection.

The first argument, the one the encyclical *Veritatis Splendor* was meant to end, concerns the compatibility of the progress of humanism with the idea of a revealed moral truth. This has been a classic question since at least the end of the eighteenth century, but one that was singularly reactivated by evolutions occurring within the very heart of the church itself. The second discussion, which once again is an old one, is symbolized by the name of the German theologian Eugen Drewermann. It has to do with the status of the interpretation of the Gospels. Should the message about Christ be read in a traditional manner as revealing incontestable historical truths, as bringing light to human beings *from the outside,* or on the contrary as a discourse with a symbolic meaning, like other myths or great poetic narratives? When we read it psychoanalytically, for example, we see that it is addressed to individuals *from within themselves.*

These two questions, as I said, even for a nonbeliever, are worth reflecting on. It may be that they are the counterpart within institutionalized religions of the process by which secular morals themselves lead us back to the idea of a spirituality we currently lack, to a "God who comes through the idea." To the divinization of the human, to that new religion of the other to which contemporary philosophy so often leads us, would correspond not only the willing humanizing of the divine, making it more intelligible to human beings and closer to them, but also a reformulating of our relation to it in terms that would no longer be arguments from authority. It is as though the internalization of spirituality were to become, for religion itself, an unavoidable requirement.

Freedom of Conscience or Revealed Truth?

Of course it is this tendency that the upholders of tradition react against. This is a comprehensible reaction if we admit that the essence of religion is exactly of a *traditional* order. Any concession to the freedom of conscience, which by nature is unlimited, represents a threat to the very idea of revelation. I cannot in good faith state that I will apply the principle of rejecting arguments from authority in one area and not in another, this far and no further. The freedom of thought is absolute or it is nothing. Here indeed is the danger that John Paul II even today, today more than ever, sees himself forced to confront. And here is where we get that "splendor" of a revealed and intangible truth that the pope believes he has to rehabilitate against the "deviations" of modernist Catholics. Here are the terms in which he defines the error that his encyclical is meant to cure:

> Certain currents in modern thought made of freedom something absolute, which then becomes the source of values. . . . In this case it is the individual conscience that decides categorically and infallibly what is good and what is evil. To the affirmation that one has to follow one's conscience is added the affirmation that a moral judgment is true because it has its origin in conscience. The inescapable claims of truth disappear, yielding their place to a criterion of sincerity, authenticity, and of "being at peace with oneself." Side by side with its exaltation of human freedom modern culture questions— oddly enough—its very existence. . . . The questions about freedom and morality cannot be separated. Though each individual has the right to be respected in his or her own journey, there remains a prior moral obligation to seek the truth.[4]

We can understand what is bothering the pope here—and sometimes, I must admit, I find it difficult to grasp why so many Christians are quick to reproach him for his "authoritarianism." The church is not a political party or a cooperative enterprise, and from the *traditional* point of view, the argument made by Jean Paul II seems as legitimate as it is on target. He poses two questions that it is difficult to see how a Christian can avoid: Can the human conscience, by itself, provide or even simply discover the source of good and evil as, indeed, the end of theological ethics seems to imply? And if one answers in the affirmative, something the church cannot do without harming itself, how is one to avoid falling into an ethics of authenticity where sincerity takes the lead over any concern for truth? The objection follows readily, and John Paul II states it: it is not enough to be sincere, to be in agreement with oneself, in order to be within the truth, which first of all and above all else requires agreement with the divine commandments. And here again I find it difficult to see what Christians can expect from the pope, on this point at least, just as I find it hard to conceive, when it comes to matters having to do with love, that the head of the Catholic Church should appeal to virtues other than fidelity.[5] Were the pope himself to make free conscience the sole criterion of truth, were the degree of conviction to become the sole support of a new moral theology, would this not come down to "the denial of the fact that God is the author of the natural moral law and not the human person"?[6]

Faced with the claims of a humanism that, according to him, leads to reexamining the very idea of a specifically Christian morality, irreducible to the ideology of human rights, the pope issues a fourfold call for a return to order:

1. The principle of theological ethics has to be reaffirmed, that is, the impossibility of calling into question the existence of "the ultimate religious foundation of moral laws" (sec. 36, p. 214). Conscience "does not establish the law, it bears witness to the authority of the natural law," for the truth is not created by human beings; it remains, today as yesterday, established by the divine law, the universal and objective norm of morality (sec. 60, p. 223).

2. This moral truth is absolute; it does not depend on circumstances or even on taking into account the consequences of our actions: "Reason attests that certain acts cannot be ordered to God: acts that are, and always will be, intrinsically evil, by reason of their very object. . . . Consequently norms that prohibit such acts oblige without any exception, and it is an error to say that one has to take into account the intention why such an act was chosen or the foreseeable consequences of such an act" (secs. 80, 81, p. 231). In philosophical terms, here the pope is denouncing both the ethics of authenticity (which confuses sincerity with truth) and utilitarianism (which relativizes the meaning of an isolated act by limiting it to its consequences).[7] What is at stake in this point is clear. It is a question of preventing Christians from giving themselves a "clear conscience" by excusing acts "contrary to truth" in the name of exceptional intentions or circumstances.

3. It therefore follows from this logic that one ought not to "model oneself on the present world." Because the current era sacralizes personal freedom does not mean it is necessary to transform the contents of Christian ethics in order to adapt it to today's tastes. On the contrary, genuine Christians are both "resisters" and

(why not?) "revolutionaries." They should transform the world rather than adapt themselves to it.

4. Finally, and this is the ultimate point of the encyclical, conscience and truth are only in appearance opposed to each other. In the terms of Vatican II, "God wanted to leave man his ability to decide." He did not take away people's freedom—just the contrary. Simply, just as God created humanity in his image, it is in following the principles of divine truth in their actions that human beings fully accede to themselves. In the language of theology, one speaks of a "participatory theonomy" (sec. 41). More clearly stated: the moral law, yes, comes from God and not from human beings (theonomy), but this does not exclude their autonomy, since human beings, somehow participating in the divine, do not reach their full liberty except through obedience to the law prescribed for them: "Genuine moral autonomy for man in no way signifies that he refuses, but rather that he welcomes the moral law, God's commandment. . . . In reality, if the heteronomy of the moral meant the negation of the self-determination of man or the imposition of norms external to his good, it would be in contradiction with the revelation of the Covenant and the redeeming Incarnation."

These responses form a coherent whole. Apart from a few reservations (to which I shall return), they do not lack for elegance or for rigor, and from a traditional point of view they seem thoroughly justified. One ought not to underestimate, however, even from a Christian perspective, the breadth and legitimacy of the movement of secularization that they, rightly, claim to remedy. Does it suffice, if we admit the breadth of this movement, to draft such an encyclical, to recall the traditional truths? I want readers to be clear about what I am saying: the question is not whether this type of response is or is not "well adapted," strategically useful, or efficacious, but rather whether it is at the level of the challenge presented by modern humanism as regards truth, not tactics.

In this respect the position defended by John Paul II suffers from certain weaknesses. We sense that as a kind of countercurrent it will not suffice to hold back the flood it means to stem. When today's Christians, even those of good will, seek to give a concrete content to this revealed moral truth that has to limit their liberty (even if only better to express it), they are referred back to the *Cate-*

chism of the Catholic Church. But this work is at times so contrary to the principles of a secular humanism, even to the teaching of the Gospels themselves, that one may doubt that participatory theonomy can leave any place for freedom of conscience. I would have expected, from reading *Veritatis Splendor,* that revelation came not to repress conscience, but to illumine and thereby to free it. But how can one attain this praiseworthy objective if the conception of truth, once made precise *in concreto,* turns out to be hostile to the very idea of conscience?

A single example, but a telling one, will make this difficulty apparent: the death penalty. I am leaving aside the fact that in the name of a traditional idea of nature homosexuality should be condemned as a mortal sin, on the same level as sex outside marriage, onanism, or medically assisted conception. We are far from the Gospel, but in the end the catechism belongs to a genre, as we well know, that is not always very subtle. But let that be. What, though, of the death penalty? How are we to legitimate the fact that the head of Roman Catholics should be able to give this content to a moral truth that he means to be "splendid"? How can he state that he recognizes "as well-founded the right and duty of legitimate public authority to punish malefactors by means of penalties commensurate with the gravity of the crime, not excluding in cases of extreme gravity, the death penalty?"[8] The principle of such a penalty not only is contrary to the "spirit of the times," it diametrically contradicts the idea, so ardently defended by John Paul II, that *intentions and circumstances cannot make an intrinsically bad act good.* Does the fact of deliberately putting another human being to death belong to that theonomy that is said to illumine the freedom of conscience? And if, in good conscience, Christians have to oppose the institutionalized church on this point, why can't they do so on other points as well that seem to them not to belong clearly to Christ's teaching?

These remarks, despite how they may appear, are not meant to add one more voice to those who denounce the teaching authority of the church. They are aimed instead at bringing out a difficulty in the notion of a participatory theonomy once we grasp its concrete meaning. For a free conscience, even that of a Christian, agrees more easily with general principles than with particular prohibitions. The stamp of humanism can be felt even at the heart

of the church, first in the very fact that it feels constrained to reestablish the primacy of truth over liberty, and second, because in
doing so it exposes itself to the criticism of the faithful, including
those who may find themselves in agreement with the general
principle of a participatory theonomy.

It is impossible, consequently, to avoid the question whether
there still exists a specifically Christian ethics—whether this does
not tend to come down to a mere surplus of faith added to what,
in the minds of most Christians, is at bottom nothing other than
the ideology of human rights. The message is a good one and no
doubt part of the historical inheritance of Christianity, at least to a
large extent. But does one still need to be a believer to share in it?
Respect for the human person and concern for others, for their
dignity or suffering, are not principles on which Christianity holds
a monopoly. For many people these principles even seem to go
against the historical inheritance of Christianity, inasmuch as the
Catholic Church has taken such a long time to free itself of coun-
terrevolutionary traditions. Whence the question, no doubt decisive for Christians, of what their faith adds to ordinary secular
morality. Far from returning to a theological ethics, it seems that
believers more and more are appropriating the secular grounds
constituted by the Declaration of the Rights of Man, and that it
is to this common stock that their faith gets grafted. It is as a surplus of meaning, therefore, in an ethical-religious mode rather a
theological-ethical one. With this shift in terms, this reversal of precedence in the relation between ethics and religion, it is clearly the
effects of humanism that are at work. And it is they, again, that
lead me to question the status of revealed truth. Nor is it by chance
that it is a problem of *interpretation* that once again confronts us,
once again a question of how subjectivity enters into the understanding of truth.

Atemporal Symbol or Historical Truth: Should We "Humanize" Christ's Message?

Are the different episodes of the life of Christ reported by the Gospels historical facts or symbols stemming from the depths of the
human soul, endowed with an atemporal significance? In the for-

mer case, they belong to the order of a truth that is both revealed and positive, that imposes itself on believers in an incontestable way; in the latter, they have to do with sphere of meaning, be it mythological or psychological, and require an interpretation.

What is at stake in this discussion is as clear as it is decisive. It is a question of deciding if the facts of religion have to preserve their status of *radical exteriority* with regard to human beings or, on the contrary, if they should be freed from their faded external finery with an eye toward internalizing their genuine meaning. And if we admit that the religious person is bound to the idea of a radical exteriority of the divine in relation to humanity, isn't its internalization a synonym for its negation? Whence an ancestral, almost visceral reserve on the part of the church with regard to historical approaches to the religious phenomenon.[9]

By appealing to the social sciences, to psychoanalysis, as well as to the comparative history of cultures, Eugen Drewermann began the debate with books whose success rapidly made it impossible for clerical authorities not to see in it a new sign of the "progress" of humanist ideology.[10] This is all the more true in that Drewermann was and remains today a Catholic priest, although in disgrace. All his work can be read as an attempt to reduce as far as possible the aspect of *exteriority* in the Christian message. It is a matter of "unalienating" religion on every level, not only institutional but also hermeneutic, so that its content should be seen as drawn from nowhere else than the depths of the human heart.

The argument over whether the truth of the Gospels is historical or symbolic thus gets inscribed in the same perspective as that taken by *Veritatis Splendor.* At issue once again is the inner freedom of conscience in relation to revelation, the process of internalizing the religious linked to the retreat of the classical figures of theological ethics. One can see why the polemics are so violent. If religion is defined by its exteriority with regard to human beings, by the fact that its revealed content, in essence, comes from elsewhere, how can applying a humanist hermeneutics that reduces it to its symbolic meanings not threaten to destroy it? Isn't it the distinction between myth and religion that such a reading tends to abolish, placing Christianity on the same level as Buddhism, Egyptian theogonies, or Greek mythology?

The central question is therefore clearly that of interpretation, and on this point Drewermann's position is clear. In an extended essay titled *De la naissance des dieux à la naissance du Christ,*[11] he tries to bring out what to his eyes is the nonfactual true significance of the "myth" of the Nativity: "The birth of the son of God is not situated at the level of history, it is situated at the level of a reality that only the images of myth are capable of describing. But it is then allowable to read the story of the birth of Jesus in Bethlehem *symbolically*" (144). And Drewermann insists on this throughout his book: we need to link these symbols to "vital experiences," to human lived experience, in order to let them act on us, like folktales and legends—that "people's poetry" in which romanticism (24) had already found its archetypes long before psychoanalysis was to show their therapeutic power. But official Catholic theology is limited to consecrating in an authoritarian manner facts that Christians are invited to believe and that, because they are external, are deprived of any genuine significance for them.

All of this will lead Drewermann to consider the virginity of Mary as a symbolic myth and not as a miraculous historical event. Mary "knew the sperm of a man," which does not prevent her, in another sense, from being a virgin. This assertion, coming from a Catholic priest, was to be judged unacceptable by the ecclesiastical authorities in the person of Monsignor Degenhardt. The record of the debate between the priest and his bishop was published and quickly translated into French (in 1993).[12] The details of this learned and scholarly discussion are not what concern us here. Drewermann had little difficulty in showing that, according to the most traditional forms of exegesis, the factuality of the affair was doubtful and that, even more, Christian faith had nothing to gain (and rather more to lose) by tying its fate to supernatural events whose credibility becomes more fragile every day. What is essential, at bottom, lies elsewhere: in the distinction Drewermann makes between history in the factual sense of the term (the German text says *Historie*) and history understood as a *narrative,* as narrative discourse (*Geschichte*), whose truth does not depend on the former sense. In this regard the virginity of Mary, like, for example, the multiplication of the loaves and fishes or other miracles, belongs to *Geschichte,* but certainly not to *Historie.* They are symbolic narra-

tives, not positive, empirical facts. We need to cite here the words
that Drewermann addressed to his bishop:

> Faith is not defined by historical [*historisch*] facts. One cannot
> draw from actual faith any hypothesis about what must have
> happened historically [*historisch*]. If historical [*historisch*] re-
> search goes against certain passages, we must be content to
> say regarding them that we do not know, or to explain what
> we can know given the framework of our present meth-
> ods. . . . Linguistically, there is a large difference between a
> historical [*historisch*] fact and history [*Geschichte*]. . . . I con-
> tinue to affirm that the multiplication of the loaves is part of
> history [*Geschichte*]! Most certainly! (83)

The bishop was highly irritated to find himself taken for a fool
on hearing that the multiplication of the loaves was a "good story"
when he wanted to be told that it was a historical fact! This is even
truer when a few lines farther along Drewermann drives home the
point by drawing on the possibilities of German:

> By history [*Geschichte*] I mean what refers to experience, to
> lived experience. This is what certain texts express in an ade-
> quate manner using formulations that are not of a historical
> [*historisch*] order. When one says "history" [*Historie*] in the
> second sense, this means that it has to be understood as infor-
> mation based on some facts. This difference has to do with
> the fact that . . . the experiences of faith are essentially of an
> inner order. We can believe this, even though we cannot say
> regarding every point that things happened in this way or
> that in observable reality. (83)

To make things more complex, or at least more complete, we
need to add that Drewermann, well aware of the danger that lies
in opposing the imaginary to the real in a straightforward and bi-
nary way, tries to introduce the existence of a third type of reality.
Let us hear what he has to add:

> For some of our audience, the problem comes from the fact
> that when we say "nonhistorical," or at least "not confirm-
> able as a fact," they understand us to be saying, "wholly

imaginary," "totally made up.". . . What we need . . . is a vision of what is real other than the one that is dominant in our modern world. . . . The truth is that there are realities that are still unclassifiable, and these are precisely religious realities.[13]

Thus between the purely imaginary and facts grasped by observation or scientific reasoning, there is supposed also to be the reality of the "symbolic" as psychoanalysis invites us to understand it. I doubt that such an assertion will reassure the bishops. In order to grasp more exactly what it is meant to say, though, we have to tie it to the overall project that was expressed in Drewermann's first writings:[14] finally to reconcile the two warring siblings, psychoanalysis and religion. What are we to make of such an undertaking, and how are we to evaluate it?

At first sight, let us say straight out, it looks like an irrational objective. Freud himself spoke to this point, and what he said is not ambiguous. In *The Future of an Illusion,* the great monotheistic religions are compared to a giant obsessional neurosis that has affected every dimension of humanity. Beyond the letter of these texts of the founding father, these two ways of looking at things seem to be irreconcilable, for one basic reason: every religion presupposes a moment of radical transcendence. The sacred, in whatever sense one takes it, refers to something external to human beings, and this is exactly why it requires an act of faith on their part. But psychoanalysis hardly admits of any exteriority other than the unconscious. Therefore if one can still speak of transcendence (of this unconscious in relation to consciousness), it would only be a matter, if we can dare put it this way, of a transcendence internal to our subjectivity. From this perspective, God and the devil can only be phantasms, the projections of unconscious conflicts. Drewermann, in all naïveté, even admits this when he states that "the devil is made up of everything that belongs to us but that we dare not live—the sum of our repressed desires and of that deeper-lying life that we repress." In short, he is nowhere other than inside us. The priest's discourse yields to that of the psychoanalyst, who may well be an atheist. And it is hard to see why what holds for the devil—that he is only a projection of *our* unconscious—should not also hold for God. Hence it is difficult to see, under these conditions, how the relation between religion and psychoanalysis can be anything other than that between fire and water.

Of course Drewermann is not unaware of all this. How does he intend to deal with the difficulty? Let us note that in the first place he refers more readily to Jung than to Freud. This is not by chance. Jung, unlike Freud, postulates the transcendence of certain "archetypes" in relation to individual subjects (for example, those associated with the image of parents, which have come down across the ages). Therefore he does not reduce everything to personal history. Drewermann is convinced that this version of psychoanalysis can add much to theology. It alone, he believes, can finally allow us to interpret the genuine significance of the biblical message.

If, as an example, we take literally the narrative in Genesis (about original sin), we run into a series of insurmountable difficulties. From a historical and scientific point of view, it can hardly make any sense for us today. All we have to do is to think of the censorious ridicule that not so long ago in the United States was applied to teaching Darwin in school. On the other hand, this narrative links up from a symbolic point of view with what we know about the origins of anxiety. Cut off from the security that faith in God's love brings, human existence, stripped of meaning, can only lose itself in various neurotic pathologies. Just as the schizophrenic experiences the absolute alienness of the world, Adam and Eve find themselves in a universe that is no longer friendly to them. As soon as God withdraws behind the indifference of nature, human beings can no longer find a safe dwelling place on this earth. In this type of comparison between a kind of anxiety with a psychic origin (that of the schizophrenic personality) and a metaphysical one of a humanity separated from God, it is no longer a question of reducing one discipline to the other. If Drewermann seeks to understand religion starting from the psychoanalytic theory of anxiety—something that leads him to deny the factual existence of the supernatural (of miracles)—he also means to elevate this theory above mere psychology, to its sacred dimension. "Theology has to correct itself and define itself in a new way . . . in the face of the perspectives opened by psychoanalysis. But conversely, the psychoanalytic vision has to accept being completed and deepened by theology, if it does not want to fall into another form of positivism."[15]

From the perspective of religion, I am not convinced that *traditional* Christian faith is not in danger, and I can see that an irreducible conflict of opinion opposes the church to Drewermann. But it is also true that his reference here to psychoanalysis does not have the feeling of a critique of religion. It stems instead, it seems to me, from the project of finally reconciling humanism and spirituality, which is concerned for both freedom of conscience and the sense of a transcendence of deeper-lying values. Purely psychological approaches to anxiety, however interesting they may be, are always too limited. That the dimension of the sacred should appear in the class of the human sciences by way of the dialogue between psychoanalysis and theology, then, can be of great interest in this regard.

Yet the conception of the divine that comes from this "psychotheology" remains marked by an extreme ambiguity,[16] which is itself quite symptomatic for new figures of the religious.

Indeed, on the one side Drewermann shares with deep ecologists the affirmation of the sacred character of all creatures. Drawing on romantic philosophers, he links up with Hans Jonas in the idea that humanity is nature's most accomplished product, that it does not differ quantitatively or qualitatively from other beings except in degree, even if this distinction confers certain special responsibilities on it. Whence his openness to Buddhism, as shown by his friendly dialogue with the Dalai Lama.[17] Whence, too, his well-known thesis about the immortality of the souls of animals[18] and, parallel to this, his no less well-known criticism of "murderous progress."[19] The work bearing this title stands in a long line of deconstructions of modern anthropocentrism. Like radical ecology, and in the same terms, it denounces one kind of monotheism, supposedly stemming from Cartesianism and the ideology of the Enlightenment, held to be largely responsible for the "devastation of the earth" in the modern period. In this respect Drewermann's book against progress offers nothing particularly new. It tends to confirm the simplistic idea that we have a choice only between a "murderous" humanism, of a Judaic and Cartesian origin, and a return to a religion of nature where every creature is situated on the same level (what ecologism designates by the expression "biospheric egalitarianism").

But as Drewermann recognizes, this pantheistic vision seems incompatible with the Christian conception of a personal God, in his splendor transcending every earthly creature. Combining Christian themes with other cosmological, Buddhist, and animist ones, which owe nothing to Christianity and even in many ways distance themselves from it, he ends up with the "nebulous mystical esotericism" that has found favor among young people ever since the sixties.[20] As in New Age ideologies, this naturalistic, impersonal conception of the divine is tied to a critique of the West. Like the latter, it goes with a radical deconstruction of the claims of the modern subject to control its fate through its own will and intelligence. In this way it can associate itself with the psychoanalytic theme of a "letting go" of the subject and plead the necessity for the individual to abandon the project of taking control of its own life through the moral conscience of the superego. If the detour through the unconscious has to be accepted, this is once and for all in order to dethrone the "metaphysical subject" held to be the master and possessor of nature as it is of itself. Whence the condemnation of "Pelagianism," then of Kantianism, and in this way of any ethics of duty meant to express the objectives of ethics in terms such as effort, imperative, law.

Through this mediation of psychoanalysis comes as well a second conception of the divine. To respond to the anxiety inherent in the solitude of human existence, we have to assume the "postulate" of a personal God who loves us, takes care of us, and gives us immortality. The question of how this image of God can be reconciled with the first one remains undealt with. But more than that, it confirms, in a way sure to disturb "traditional" Christians, Voltaire's saying that in trying to make God an answer to human expectations, we risk reducing him to a mere projection of our needs. This fear is all the more justified in that it fits perfectly with a reading of the Gospels in symbolic and not historical terms. From Feuerbach to Freud, passing through Marx, the most virulent criticism of religion has taken just this form. It is nothing other than a "fetishized" human creation, in the sense Marx gave to this concept. We have produced the idea we needed and, forgetting this process of production, we yield to the illusion of the objective existence of what we have produced.

Yet it remains true that in this humanization of the divine, so earnestly sought by Drewermann, we have one of the most fundamental exigencies of the secular universe, which, if not satisfied, at least does get taken into account: a spirituality compatible with that freedom of conscience and autonomy that the refusal of arguments from authority invites us to think through. In this sense religion enters the orbit of one of the moral visions that dominates the contemporary universe: an ethics of "authenticity" and of a care for the self that will sacralize human existence to the point that it will come to sum up the divine, which will no longer appear under the heading "heteronomy," henceforth identified with "dogmatism." It is no longer in terms of some grandiose ending, situated radically outside human beings, that we are to seek the divine, but in that love that is within us all. "Only love," writes Drewermann, "believes in immortality. We can learn this only along with a person whom we love as he or she loves us. One can get to heaven only in twos."[21] This message, like a real earthquake, has to upset the institutional church. Especially because to this humanization of the divine in theology, in contemporary society there corresponds the humanization of evil.

The Metamorphoses of the Devil

What is there left for Satan to do at the end of this century, on the threshold of "year 2000," carrying the lovely promises that were those of the Enlightenment: the progress of civilization based on science and technology, reason at last victorious over superstition, freedom of thought emancipated from clerical authority, perpetual peace? Hasn't the devil disappeared from our beliefs to the point where even most Christians see in him only a metaphorical image? Up to the beginning of the eighteenth century, when Catholics recited the Lord's Prayer they begged the Most High to deliver them from "the evil one." At least that is what they said. Significantly, the formula has disappeared from this famous prayer, having been transformed, or so to speak humanized, almost as though, in parallel to the secularization of the divine, that of the demon has also occurred. Modern believers ask God only to deliver them from "evil." This is the first metamorphosis of the devil. His personification has vanished over time.

And yet nothing has really changed. A simple reference to what happened in Rwanda or Bosnia yields the irrepressible sense that if the devil is dead, we are far from having finished with the demonic. Of course there is quite a difference between doing something "bad" and doing evil. The distinction is not a new one. Plato had already pointed out that the physician must sometimes inflict pain on the patient, without this giving any hint of evil intentions on his part. In truth, like his teacher Socrates, Plato doubted that human beings could intentionally do wrong, that they could deliberately adopt it as their project. And it is just this suspicion that still today makes us uneasy. For it is not the mere sight of wrongdoing by others that takes away our words and our appetite so much as the fact of our having a conviction, whose underlying motives we cannot make sense of, that the calamities that fall on human beings seemed chosen as such, almost for themselves. It is as though there exists a logic of hate,[22] far surpassing any identification of those initially "responsible" for a conflict, whatever it may be. Rapes, gratuitous killings, massive massacres, and the most sophisticated types of tortures are commonplace in the camps of the executioners and before long, if the opportunity should arise, even among the victims. I say this not to deny the political responsibilities of those who should be held accountable but to emphasize that what is most surprising, for us who have been raised in the relative calm of peaceful societies, is that such acts are not exceptional, that they have become the norm, and that they find, in the end and on all sides, so many individuals to take part in them.

What is strange is that sometimes (always?) these hideous crimes seem alien to the ends of war properly speaking. Why, in order to attain victory, was it necessary to force mothers to throw their living babies into a concrete mixer, as we are assured was the case in Bosnia?[23] Why behead infants with a machete to prop up cases of beer or split their skulls in front of their parents as the Hutus did? Why torture your enemy before executing him, if he is to be executed? That the soldier, even more than Plato's physician, must "do wrong," we will all agree. This is why war is so hateful in principle. But short of this extreme case, incontestably more desperate than that of medicine, there is no necessity, strictly speaking, to "do wrong" in order to gain victory. There is, even within the most tragic, most brutal conflict, an ethics of the soldier, who is not required to be a thoroughly rotten bastard in order to do a dirty job. Heroism, courage, but also the spirit of chivalry, even of compassion, can preserve a place.

It is as though war provides the occasion for slipping imperceptibly, with impunity, from the bad to the evil, as though wrongdoing is no longer a means but an end, no longer a tragic reality but a pastime, not to say a thrilling venture. Hence it is not by chance or out of superstition that theology spoke of "malice." Kant himself, who shared Socrates' ideas without always acknowledging them, thought it was due to the devil. One of his disciples, Benjamin Erhard, went so far as to imagine, in an unusual little work titled *Apology of the Devil*, what the principles of action would be for a being who would chose to carry out, without second thoughts or any hesitation, only evil actions. These principles could well be those of the Anti-Christ.

Even today, particularly in its struggle against "modernist" Catholics concerned to accommodate Christianity to the taste of the day, the church is firm in maintaining its dogma. The devil possesses a real existence. However much it may displease Drewermann and other theologians won over by psychoanalysis, the Adversary is not some symbol to be interpreted, a psychic entity produced by our unconscious, but definitely the prince of demons, if not in flesh and blood, since he is a spirit, at least sufficiently powerful to become incarnate in a human body, there to engender the quite tangible phenomenon of "possession." Therefore there is nothing superfluous about the practice of exorcism, however archaic it may seem.[24] At least this is what we are reminded of by a document from the Sacred Congregation published in 1975 with the title "Christian Faith and Demonology." It is also what Paul VI himself emphasized in a discourse dated 15 November 1972: "Whoever does not admit the existence of the demon or who considers him to be an independent phenomenon, unlike any other creature, not having God as his origin, or who again defines him as a pseudoreality, as a conceptual and fantastic personification of

the unknown origins of our maladies, transgresses biblical and ecclesiastical teaching."

Therefore, against Manichaeans and the disciples of Zoroaster,
we are to maintain the idea that it was indeed God, and no other,
who created the devil—otherwise there would be two equal principles and the divine would no longer be the "Almighty." But in
order not to attribute to the Lord the creation of evil, which would
be a sacrilege, it is also necessary to admit that Satan, a sublime
angel in the beginning, owes his maliciousness only to himself and
to his free choice of evil.[25]

Despite the pope's efforts, the Adversary has come down to
earth. The humanization of the divine, the internalization of religious content by the human spirit, was also the internalization of
evil. Always quick to grasp the flaws within history, Rousseau was
among the first to comprehend and formulate this. "Man, seek the
author of evil no longer," he wrote in *Émile*. "It is yourself. No evil
exists other than that which you do or suffer, and both come to
you from yourself."[26] This secularization has occurred, and the
words of the church are less and less convincing. However, radical
evil was not content to pass from the demonic to the human, from
a spiritual being to a carnal one. A second metamorphosis has also
taken place. The demonic seems today to have quit the personal
sphere in general, no longer being imputable to a subject, of whatever order, but only to a context—to the social, family, or other
setting that is held to have engendered it. It is not certain, despite
appearances, that such "progress" brought about by reason against
superstition is unequivocal. Even Hannah Arendt, so little suspect
of any sympathy for the determinism of the social sciences, came
up with the idea of a "banality of evil."[27] A conscientious small-
time bureaucrat, good father and husband, Adolf Eichmann is said
to have carried out his task "without a thought," in an instrumental, mechanical way, as if it were any ordinary undertaking. I am
convinced of the contrary, and having reflected on it, I wonder if
here again theology has not reached another truth more profound
than that of our contemporary talk in denouncing the maliciousness of a personified entity and in attributing the will to do evil as
such to a conscious subject. I do not claim that the mystery of evil
is dissipated in this way, but at least it is named and it remains a

question, even for nonbelievers. Baudelaire said of the devil that his greatest trick is to persuade us he does not exist. Everything suggests that this trick has worked, that he has convinced us.

The Dehumanization of Evil or the Reduction to Context: Lawyer's Talk

When a particularly horrible crime is the talk of the town—a crime such as can occur even among us, yes, but one like those that get organized regularly on a large scale when there is a war—lawyers willingly declare themselves disciples of the social sciences. Sociological or psychoanalytic explanations readily impose themselves in establishing extenuating circumstances. Then it is a question of pointing to the "difficult past" of a murderer, who quickly becomes the victim of society, or to a social setting, or a family, or a genetic heritage, or even a political power said to have fabricated him. The argument is so ritual, so codified, that of itself it leads to derision. Like the lawyer who in defending a son accused of murdering his parents exclaimed to the jury, "What, are you going to condemn an orphan!" If we smile at this joke, it is, as always, because it says more than one might think. In fact it says almost too much, for all the social sciences—that is, what is essential (in quantity at least) about today's talk devoted to human existence—are evoked in this little joke. Here we have the ultimate metamorphosis of the devil. Against those religions that situate evil in a personal transcendent being, but also against the humanism of Rousseau, who was content to displace evil toward humanity at the risk of demonizing the latter, the social sciences add a supplementary step to the secularization of evil. It is in terms of some context, some "social setting," as one so nicely puts it, that they invite us to look today. As though human beings, who at bottom are not responsible for their acts, were only ever the product of a series of intersecting histories: those of their class and nation, of their family and culture, or again, with the arrival on the market of "sociobiology," of their genes and hormones. And the intellectual device thereby set in place functions so well that evil, in the last instance, is nowhere to be found.

Whence our feeling of a great gap between what we observe

and what we are capable of thinking—an abyss separating the almost daily reality of the horror that surrounds us from the concepts that, in claiming to grasp it, reduce it to nothingness. An abyss that is all the more enigmatic for us democrats in that it possesses deeper roots than our modern representations of human existence.

Fascinated by equality, our democratic societies have had in effect to reject—which is not bad in all ways—the idea that there exists an aristocracy of good and evil. "Men are born free and with equal rights." And if these rights are to find some equivalent in concrete facts, we have to suppose that one is not born irremediably good or bad, but that one becomes so as a function of one's circumstances. The idea of someone "bad" by nature repulses us, and this is also why, believing that nothing is ever done for all eternity or even all the time, we have ended up abolishing the death penalty, which clearly leaves few opportunities for the criminal to rehabilitate himself. It was the same way of looking at things that led to the elaboration of conceptual instruments meant to reduce evil to determining situations that almost mechanically produce it. It is true that in this way things become more intelligible, less mysterious, and less disturbing to us because they are explicable in terms of a chain of causation. But at the very moment when we believe we have identified the reason, it slips through our fingers: engendered by a history *external* to the individual, it cannot, definitively, be imputed to anyone.

This procedure of reduction to some form of determinism has many faces today. It constitutes the dominant ideology to such an extent that some, in the name of the social sciences, have been led to "banalize" the most incontestable figures of contemporary evil. Nazism, for example, which for our collective imagination figures at the summit of the disasters of this century. In Germany, during the seventies, this led to polemics of a rare virulence. We need to dwell on it for a moment, because it can serve as a paradigm of what is at issue.

Out of a concern to get beyond the stage of mere moral indignation, some historians turned to sociology to try finally to understand, or rather explain, how Hitler came to put in place the "final solution." The hypothesis of madness seemed insufficient to them, too personal at bottom to account for such a wide-ranging social and political phenomenon. Therefore they sought to bring to light the *mechanisms* through which the political system of the Third Reich could have *given rise to* genocide, hence to lay bare the *context and mode of production* of such a crime against humanity. Hans Mommsen and Martin Broszat, to name them, are progressive liberals bound by no sympathy, even unconscious, that links them to the ideology of Nazism.[28] On the contrary, they continually emphasize the aversion it arouses in them. Both are excellent historians, acknowledged as such by their colleagues. Yet—and this is the heart of the matter—turning to the social sciences naturally pushes one, unless one stays on guard, toward banalization. In demonstrating the wheels of National Socialist power by analyzing the ferocious competition between different groups, the fragmented decision making, and so on, Mommsen and Broszat bit by bit lay out a unique portrait of Hitler—that of a "weak dictator," not responsible for political choices that were the effect of innumerable microdecisions and slight shifts determined in a quasi-mechanical way by the functioning of German political life. In short, there is an absolute victory of context over the responsibility of human actors, since the only guilty party, in the final analysis, is nothing other than the system—that is, no one! If this thesis caused a scandal, let me say again, it was not because it was reproached for being false but, on the contrary, because it was thought to be true enough to legitimate trivializing the crime. By demonstrating that it was determined from the outside, with implacable rigor and independent of any stated *intentions* of the politicians, one takes all responsibility away from people by situating it in an abstract entity. In this way Mommsen and Broszat confirmed Arendt's thesis of the "banality of evil."

Against such an analysis built with the aid of sociology,[29] other historians[30] therefore saw the necessity to rehabilitate the will and the role of leading actors, even if they were, as in this case, great criminals. It is not so much the mechanisms of politics one has to consider as those "stated intentions" that sociology seeks to do without. It is in the worldview of the Nazi leaders, in their *Weltanschauung*, that we can already read a sinister future that in the end will turn out to confirm its dire premises. These historians, as one can well imagine, were charged with conservatism, with archaic resistance to the progress of scientific knowledge.

I make no claim here to settle this argument. I want only to underscore one of the factors that was at stake, one perceptible even to the broader public. The "scientific" approach to the human world, what Dilthey called a "world of spirit" in order to protect it from the natural sciences, tends toward objectivity. This term has to be taken in the strong sense. Taken as an object, human existence is reified, transformed into a mere thing, and human behavior, be it good or bad, even malicious, is, after being analyzed, nothing more than the result of an unconscious, blind mechanism. Yes, the lawyer who makes such a plea wins. His discourse is powerful because in the end he is armed with strong arguments to confirm the Socratic adage: No one, it has now been proved, does wrong voluntarily! But the world of spirit thereby loses something, and we no longer understand what opposes humanitarian action, in the broadest sense of the term, to those acts we judge to be "inhuman." To the extent that the responsibility for wrongdoing is taken from us, we are thereby, and for the same reasons, relieved of the responsibility for doing good. If no one does wrong voluntarily, if everything is determined by its context, neither is anyone good any more, except by the effect of some favorable situation. Human responsibility vanishes, and good and evil go with it. The metamorphoses of the devil may finally be completed. His cunning has clearly carried the day.

May we still doubt this, even if everything else may be opposed to our doing so? Undoubtedly, the interpretations suggested by sociology and the other social sciences have their truth. Who today would deny that our social or emotional environment, to say nothing of our genetic heritage, plays a conscious or unconscious role in our behavior? Still, the suspicion arises that these scientific considerations are always incomplete, that they always leave out something (essential?) from what they claim to grasp exhaustively. It is wrong, to put it in a formula, to confuse a *situation*, which may favor some kinds of behavior without necessarily determining them, with a *determination* that would engender them in a mechanistic and irresistible way. How can anyone seriously believe that those who decide to raise rape and torture to the level of political principles do not know what they are doing? How can anyone accept that in so doing they become no longer executioners, but victims of a "difficult" upbringing? We can admit, strictly speaking, that the brutes filled with alcohol who carry out such dirty deeds are motivated by poorly controlled sadistic impulses, nationalist propaganda, or the effects of drugs that affect the brain. We can even say that one of these drugs, used by Russian troops in Chechnya, bore the apt label "ferocine." All of this is possible. But what of those who prescribed this "ferocine," who planned massacres from their offices, who hinted at the order to level a village, knowing what this would mean in the field? Isn't the hypocrisy with which they deny having used such means what an old saying calls the homage vice renders to virtue? To explain their behavior by a disturbance in their libido or a difficult childhood is pathetic with regard to the political scale of this phenomenon. But to turn instead to sociological explanations runs up against the problem of the mystery of diversity. Not every Serb has given in to national communism, any more than the Croatians are unanimous in seeing themselves in their fascist-leaning leaders. Every situation, it is true, can have an effect. But none by itself is strictly determining. This is proved by the existence, however marginal, of dissidents and resisters in every totalitarian regime.

Furthermore, it is a happy fact that some representatives of the social sciences have enough good sense and intellectual courage to acknowledge this. But they have to stand against the dominant currents that constitute their disciplines. Notably, one of the tendencies of psychoanalysis has clearly been toward the most radical kind of reductionism. Freud himself did not escape this. As regards the personification of evil, he mostly has only platitudes to tell us. The devil is the unconscious, the "counterwill," libido, sex, repressed instincts, a bad father, and other such discoveries suitable for a first-year introductory course. For example, there is this letter to Fliess of January 1897: "I have found the explanation why witches fly; their broom is probably the great lord Penis." Nicely put, but the hidden thread cannot remain overlooked forever. Once Freud introduces the mechanism of "projection" and above all the death instinct into his reflections, undoubtedly he gets closer to the question. But nevertheless the mystery remains, for evil is not a mere emanation from the mind, a purely psychic mechanism. It depends on something external and real, as one of today's better analysts, André Green, recognizes, not without a certain humility. Green concludes an important article significantly bearing the title "Why Evil?" in a way worth reflecting on: "I remain convinced that evil exists, and that it is not a defense mechanism or a protective facade, or the camouflage for a psychosis. We have to seek out evil where it holds sway. In the external world. . . . I have tried to show that without our knowing it, or paying attention to it, we are assaulted not just by violence, a trivial assertion, but by evil. Sociological or political rationalizations can propose their explanations. When we test them out, they don't work." Referring to those victims of the Shoah whom fate allowed to survive, Green adds this: "Everything indicates from their testimony that they have not ever been able to make sense of it. And we even less."[31]

Hence evil lacks a "why." This answer will dismay those committed to science. However, it is not as trivial as it may seem. It suggests that the mystery of evil lies, in Kant's formulation, in the depths of the human soul. Above all, it signifies that there *must be* a mystery of evil, as also of good, if these two terms that are constitutive of the very idea of morality are to be able to receive a meaning. Both are excessively baroque in relation to the logic of nature. Comparison with the animal kingdom is singularly illumining about this. Animals are not properly speaking bad even when they inflict the most terrible suffering on their fellows (and examples are abundant of "cruelty" in the animal world), any more than they are really capable of that unexpected—I was going to say heaven-sent—generosity that is sometimes seen among humans. However devoted or affectionate they may seem to be, everything in their behavior is predictable and rule governed, not to say unavoidable. But human beings are, par excellence, beings of antinature or, to put it a better way, the only natural beings (for we too are animals) who not only are not programmed by this nature but can oppose themselves to it.[32] Here lies the mystery of our freedom understood as our capacity to transcend the natural cycle of instinctual life. "Excess" is another way of saying transcendence. If good and evil are mysterious, and sometimes as unexpected as they are incomprehensible, it is because they have to be so in order to exist. It is because they are not moved by this mysterious freedom, this incomprehensible independence with regard to nature, that automatons, and even animals, are incapable of either good or evil. They are determined by a mechanism or an instinct to live and behave according to intangible and immutable laws that are the laws of their species over the millennia. Humans, on the contrary, are not programmed by any code. As Rousseau noted, a human being escapes the supreme law of nature, that of self-preservation, to such an extent that he can commit suicide, can sacrifice himself, can commit excessive acts that lead to losing his life! And Fichte added, it is in his eye that one can see that fundamental indetermination implying a freedom that, endlessly, can choose to be free for good or free for evil. Unlike a bird's eye, which looks like a mirror, the human eye, by some inexplicable quality, allows itself to be penetrated by the other's look and shows itself as bearing a meaning that no one decides a priori. Kant spoke of an unfathomable mystery of human freedom, but a necessary one. For the same reasons it is impossible to praise apart from the possibility of blaming, moral good is inseparable from the possibility of evil, that is, from that mysterious postulate that humans, in the final analysis, do possess an unfathomable freedom of choice.

Don't we say that wicked behavior is "inhuman"? We even go so far as to ridicule it and misuse the exact sense of the word by declaring it "bestial." What a blunder—not only is evil human, it is one of the characteristics of human beings, one of our most specific differences from other beings. Among the beasts there are no murders. On the other hand, in Ghent, Belgium, there is a strange, disturbing museum: the museum of torture. There one finds innumerable instruments meant to inflict on other human beings the greatest sufferings one can invent. What is striking in this sinister setting is the inexhaustible richness of the human imagination when it comes to doing harm. Alexis Philonenko has tried to describe it.[33] He correctly concludes that it is, alas, human, all too human. Here we see the absolute enigma of evil, the why of the uneasiness evil raises for any philosophical reflection. It is through humans that we apprehend that it is inflicted on other humans. To the figure of the man-God there corresponds that of the man-devil.

Between religion, which represented the demonic through the features of a personified entity, and the social sciences, which tend purely and simply to eliminate it, there appears a third order of discourse: in the strongest sense of the term, it humanizes the mystery of evil, that is, internalizes it, without claiming to be done with the matter. Whence the urgency and difficulty of moral reactions, be they humanitarian or otherwise, that give rise to the perception of evil as such. Is ethics, once secularized, still capable of finding within itself the necessary strength to carry the struggle through to victory? Or, on the contrary, are we living, as an unavoidable effect of the humanization of the divine, in a "postduty" era, marked by the end of any great ardor or decisive commitment in favor of the good? The question needs to be asked.

CHAPTER TWO

The Divinization of the Human

THE SECULARIZATION OF ETHICS AND
THE BIRTH OF MODERN LOVE

At the end of the century, sometimes not without ostentation, we like to place ourselves under the flattering auspices of a "return to ethics." In striking contrast to the surrounding atmosphere, the discourse of values is everywhere: in the rejuvenation of charitable organizations, in the struggles against racism and "exclusion," in the call for a more rigorous professional ethics on the part of the media, in a moralizing of economic and political life, in concern for the environment, in an increased power of judges, in bioethics, in the struggle to protect the rights of minorities and prevent sexual harassment, in campaigns against smoking. The list of these new imperatives is endless, which, it seems, makes credible the idea of a new and general preoccupation with the good, if not the idea of an "avenging angel." [1]

Yet in spite of all this, some will reply that a pure, hard-nosed ethics, that of the agonizing categorical imperative, is nowhere to be found. The rhetoric of austere obligations, the philosophy of "you must, therefore you can," of strict republicanism, long ago burned out, giving way to the individualistic logic of competition, consumption, and happiness—in short, to a demand for authenticity, for the self-satisfaction we ironically call "ethics." The end of moral norms rooted in the strict universe of a revealed religion or even in that of a mere secular understanding of citizenship is said to indicate, in the end, if not the advent of laxity, at least the dissolution of any notions of effort and sacrifice to the profit of universal egoism. Just consider how cowardly the democracies are when it comes to defending their own principles! Look at the rise of corporatism, the loss of any sense of civic responsibility on the part of many ordinary citizens,[2] and at the highest level, the multiplication of "scandals." Here as elsewhere the "lowest level" seems to be the rule. Concern for oneself, for one's own well-being and that of those nearest to one, unbridled competition, the striving for material and psychological comfort are said to have replaced the old requirement for giving of oneself, through an erosion of the feeling of any sense of radical dependence on the divine or the nation. The truth of secular ethics can be read in this "twilight of duty" that the modern world, as a universe of competition and consumption, offers us as a permanent spectacle.

Moral Progress or the "Twilight of Duty"?

What then do we have—decline or a return of ethics, moral progress or the sinking of humanity into individualism and infinite consumption? This argument, like that about modern culture, continues to haunt contemporary thought. It is relaunched every publishing season by new books that try to add their decisive contributions but end up relativizing the optimism of those who uphold the idea of a "moral generation."

At the origin of these legitimate questions lies the appearance in the sixties of a vision of the world characterized by a claim to "authenticity" and, in the name of respect for individuals, calling for the eradication of every form of dogmatism, whether of religious or moral origin. According to Gilles Lipovetsky the advent of such an ethics, far from being a superficial episode limited to the decade of the sixties, marked the end of a long process of secularization leading, from the eighteenth century, toward full secularism.[3] The new demands for individual autonomy represent the downfall of the sacrificial ideals that still dominated the first secular, strict republican moralities. His diagnosis is worth reflecting on, not just because it is intrinsically interesting, but also because, almost in advance, he denies the idea that any new figures of the sacred might be able to organize contemporary values. If what is said is to stop sounding like slogans, no doubt we need to define the category of authenticity more concretely.

The Ethics of Authenticity

In the first place, it overlaps that antiaristocratic demand that so clearly appears in the protest movements of the sixties. The old world, the political universe that the French Revolution sought to break away from, was dominated through and through by the idea of hierarchy. Of beings, yes (this was the basis of feudalism), but also of norms—divine ones being held to be superior to any human kind. There has been no democratic movement over the past two centuries that has not insisted on the necessity of promoting equality and secularity. May 1968 was no exception. Yet by all evidence social, political, moral, aesthetic, and cultural hierarchies continue to impose themselves on everyone (or almost everyone). This is what the ethics of authenticity denounces most of all. As was seen during the sixties, it meant to promote, against the old notion of excellence, the goal of an absolute equalization of values and conditions. One highly symbolic example will suffice to make this clear: there is no difference to be drawn between "good" and "bad" sexual practices. That is the meaning of the much talked about liberation demanded by young people. Here as elsewhere, let's be done with any normative, "repressive" notion of hierarchy. There is no longer any norm—natural, religious, juridical, or whatever—only the demand, itself perceived as the only authentically moral one, to let all people be themselves, just as long as they truly do so. This is why the egalitarian motif, understood as everyone's right to authenticity, so easily gets associated with the idea of a "right to be different." In the cultural arena this watchword finds a number of equivalent expressions: every "distinction" has to be abolished between classical and "pop" music, between the traditional novel and the "comic book," between the European West and the people of the Third World; in short, anything that it would be wrong to deal with in terms of the still aristocratic categories of "high" and "low" culture. It is not a question here of judging this universal claim to equality through authenticity (through the right to be oneself), but only of determining what is specific and novel about it in relation to traditional ethics of duty. Moreover, it is easy to see that it contains both better and worse forms, as is typical of so many modern currents of history.

I come therefore to the second characteristic feature of this new ethics: its antimeritocratic claim. In "bourgeois morality"—a heading under which we all too quickly include any reference to an imperative of duty—the structure was always the same: there exists a general norm, transcending individuals in their particularity (for example, school curricula in our French republicanism). And moral effort consisted in getting as close as possible to this ideal, which was somehow external to oneself. Even if the notion of autonomy of the subject was not rejected, it was thought of as a distant objective, difficult to attain, not as a current reality. Effort and merit were inseparable, the latter being at bottom only the outcome of the former. Transcendence of the norm, a tension in the will, a self-ideal, these are the governing terms that, not so long ago, defined the moralities of duty—in truth, for most people, morality per se.

Once it is "forbidden to forbid," once any normativity is perceived as repressive, individuals become their own norms to and for themselves. Here once again, the claim for authenticity rings out: "Be yourself," it commands, showing that some small imperative remains to be uttered. And again, the right to be different goes along with this. With everyone from now on having to become what he is, and "being yourself" receiving the stamp of a new legitimacy, one cannot judge a priori the differences the process will bring up in the end. What is essential is to be done with the transcendence of norms, finally to reach a right comprehension of this indubitable fact: the only transcendence that remains is that of oneself over oneself, that of an authentic ego over an inauthentic one. In short, a transcendence wholly circumscribed within the sphere of self-immanence of the individual ego. And from here follows, in order to close the distance thus marked out, the invention of techniques or practices that will open the way to authenticity: sports activities, beginning with jogging (a mass phenomenon, unique of its kind, it should be emphasized), allowing one "to be at home in one's body," just as a galaxy of new therapies, derived from psycho-analysis or Eastern wisdom, allow one to "be at home in one's head."

The Secularization of Ethics: Eclipse of the Sacred?

In this way the ethics of authenticity wipes out what the first secular moralities had been able to preserve from the past. Even though apparently freed of any theological reference, they nonetheless maintained an element of religiousness: the sacred and intangible character of duty, the idea of a radical dependence of human existence with regard to certain transcendent norms remained theological in essence, even when secularized.

The first cycle of secularization therefore is said to have as its principal characteristic "that in emancipating itself from the spirit of religion, it borrowed one of its principal figures: the notion of an infinite debt, of an absolute duty."[4] Kantian rigor and republican patriotism are good examples. In both traditions (which by the way are closely connected), self-sacrifice and the struggle against individual egoism were valued above all else, even when the values of secularism, such as anticlericalism, were strongly proclaimed.

> In bringing to its maximum refinement the ethical ideal, in professing the cult of secular virtues, in magnifying the obligation of personal sacrifice on the altar of the family, the fatherland, or history, modern thinkers did not so much break with the moral tradition of self-renunciation that followed from the religious schema of an unlimited imperative for duty as transfer the higher obligations toward God to the profane human sphere; they were transformed into unconditional duties toward oneself, toward others, toward the collectivity. The first cycle of modern morality functioned like a religion of secular duty.[5]

The principal hypothesis of this analysis is that the austere, heroic, sacrificial phase of democratic societies is gone for good. Since the 1950s we have entered a second age of secularization where the ethics of authenticity has been elaborated—the "postduty" era. "The 'it is necessary' has given way to the incantation of happiness, the categorical obligation to the stimulation of the senses." Today we live with a "new logic of the process of secularization of ethics . . . that no longer consists in affirming ethics as a sphere independent of revealed religions, but in socially dissolving its religious form: duty itself." With the consequence that "for the first time, behold a society that, far from exalting higher commandments, euphemizes them and deprives them of any believability, that devalues the ideal of abnegation by systematically stimulating immediate desires, the passion of the ego, intimate and materialistic happiness. . . . In being organized essentially apart from the form of duty, ethics will henceforth accomplish in its full radicality the age of the 'end of religion' (Marcel Gauchet)." Whence the rise in demands for authenticity, for the right to be oneself, apart from any imposition of values external to oneself. In "postmoralist" societies, therefore, "the label 'ethics' is pervasive but the requirement for commitment nowhere . . . the reigning ethics calls for no major sacrifice, no self-uprooting."[6]

Ought we to despair over this? Not at all, according to Lipovetsky, who here rejoins the fundamental intuition of the first theoreticians of liberalism: it is not through puritan incantations to abnegation that the common good is most likely to be realized, but through a logic of rightly understood interests, which to be sure is not sacrificial. This is a painless logic, since it requires no self-sacrifice for the other. Examples that reinforce the theoretical argument are not lacking. Consider the case of Perrier. When this well-known firm discovered that a few bottles of its water had been contaminated by an undesirable chemical, it immediately decided to withdraw every bottle in circulation. The cost of this operation? 200 million francs. An example of a generous sacrifice? Not at all, for the result was beneficial in terms of "communication." It allowed the company to preserve, even to reinforce, its image of purity. Thus it is through interest, not through some heroic respect for values, that the common good gets realized. Or think of the example of campaigns in favor of some foreign land where war, oppression, or famine reigns. The bag of rice our children bring to school to aid the children of Somalia constitutes the perfect illustration. It costs them nothing, either in time or in money. Provided by their parents, for whom it represents a tiny expense, it gives everyone a good conscience without requiring anything of them. Requiring no self-sacrifice, the action is nonetheless "objectively" good. It can even claim to be useful and, extended to a broader scale, as was the case with the Telethon or some other forms of humanitarian aid, it may even ease suffering and save many lives. Proof, if proof is needed, that the good can be realized without pain and without thereby losing its fundamental qualities. Certainly a small number of activists are devoted, but not the general public. It is through interest, knowledge, or even the media that the good will most surely be realized, there where the old ideology of duty turned out more than once to be deadly. Die for my country, die for ideas? Why not instead live for them, in a peaceful, reasonable, and, overall more efficacious way than in the times of religious or secular abnegation?

The conclusion is obvious: the alleged "return to ethics" will not be one if we mean by this a resurgence of the ethics of duty. Apart from a few vague desires, the charitable values of devotion to the other occupy only a tiny place over against the empire of egoism, consumer consumption, and well-being. There is a perfect harmony between the ethics of authenticity, which reduces everything to our own attainment of our own truth, and the ethics of "rational calculation," which counts more on the logic of interests than on any virtuous goodwill. They are two faces of the same reality. They combine, to the point of becoming one, in their common opposition to aristocratic and meritocratic ethics, in their concern at last to do justice to the legitimate requirements of democratic individualism.

We have to admit, the cardinal hypothesis is strong that the present, marked by the secularization of ethics, is a time of the "twilight of duty." It insightfully relativizes the superficial idea of a "return to ethics." It can even be illustrated by a large number of concrete facts. However, I would like to suggest a different interpretation, one that sees a future evolution other than a pure and simple "disenchantment," even were this to be in some ways a healthy development.

Toward a Sacralization of the Human

First, by way of diagnosis, I am convinced that we do not live today in a "postduty" era. One might even hold, beyond appearances, that it is in the most secularized universe that the notion of duty attains its full truth. The definition of virtue as disinterested action, as an uprooting of the individual's natural egoism, seems to me, over against what Lipovetsky proposes, more sure than ever in our representations of true morality. This clearly does not mean we are always, or even often, at the ideal level. What is more, whether we live in a time that is more or less "virtuous" than past periods is one of those questions that in essence are undecidable and that depend above all on the attitude of anyone claiming to make such a judgment. On the other hand, a moment of self-reflection will suffice to make us recognize that what Perrier did, or a check sent to the Telethon, or even the schoolchild's bag of rice does not inspire great moral admiration. In the best of cases, we find all that clever or even nice, but no more. In truth, we doubt the sacrificial or disinterested character of such actions, and this doubt continues for each of us, perhaps unconsciously or without thinking, to hold as a moral criterion. Let me go even further in this direction. The personalities most dear to the French who regularly are asked to give their opinion are for the most part so for reasons stemming from a "meritocratic" and sacrificial ethic, because we attribute to them an exceptional capacity of devotion to some cause serving the common interest. This is as true for Mother Teresa or Sister Emmanuelle as for the organization Doctors of the World or for Abbé Pierre. I can already hear the objection: not everyone is that disinterested, some even show too pronounced a taste for being before the microphones or on television. But that confirms my point. Who does not see by means of such suspicions—whether they are justified or not doesn't really matter here—that it is still the ideal of a disinterested virtue that gets expressed in this way? Moreover, it is such notions that shape our whole judicial system. Our criminal law, in particular, rests wholly on the ideas of merit and responsibility. What would be the sense of expressions such as "extenuating circumstances" or, aggravating matters, "premeditation" if we did not presume a capacity of choice in every individual (provided he is of "sound mind"), some power to rise above our natural inclinations in order to respect the law rather than infringe it, and if we did not make good and evil depend directly on such a capacity?

Perhaps some will accept these comments, only to submit them to a second objection. The personalities referred to are exceptions that confirm the rule. They make us think of those heroes whose uniqueness we salute, if only better to excuse ourselves from the duty of having to imitate them. In everyday life, any concern for sacrifice has surely given way to concern for security and happiness. The check we send to the Telethon only amounts to a simple, banal way to get rid of our guilt. Therefore in the sphere of ideas, and by way of a few idealized personalities, meritocratic virtue still gets expressed. But only as something left over, without any real basis in fact. Look at Bosnia or, closer to home and even plainer, the fate of the homeless among us. We feel a bit of sadness, but from a distance, and this pain, however sincere it may be, remains, for the great majority of us (for all those who don't make it their job, and not only them), quite bearable.

Maybe, even undoubtedly, such assertions coincide with a nonnegligible part of our ordinary experience (even if, it seems to me, they underestimate the significance and importance of the great growth in charitable organizations—something I shall return to). However, they miss the heart of the question. For social conditions as well as the meaning of sacrificial action have changed radically with the advent of secular individualism. Self-sacrifice is no longer today imposed from the outside but is freely consented to and felt as an *inner* necessity—this is what is essential. This is the ever more visible consequence of the growth of individual autonomy. It is no longer a question of dying for your country with a flower attached to your rifle and a smile on your lips (if this was ever the case—but in the end, as no one will deny, patriotism was once a reality). It is true that sending a check to the Telethon brings no threat where we live. But let us reflect for a moment on the other factor that needs to be taken into consideration. The only one making us do this is the person who signs the check. What then are we to say about those who, for reasons that we can indeed laugh at or suspect, commit a part of their lives, their free time, and for a few, their whole life, to charitable action, even when no pressure other than an inward one constrains them to do so?

However we look at this, we are forced to acknowledge that such devotion is no longer the obligatory result of age-old traditions. It does not depend on any irresistible communal emotion; rather, for the first time perhaps in the history of humanity, it has to find its exclusive source in human beings themselves. In other words, we live in a time of passing from a logic of heterosacrifice to one of autosacrifice. It is not surprising, under these conditions, if we notice that devotion takes a more gentle form than formerly. What is happening, behind the apparent "twilight of duty," will attain the reality of its concept, its truth, only at the moment when the reign of heteronomy finally ends.

The Humanization of Sacrifice

Modernity is not so much rejecting transcendence as rearranging it to fit conditions stemming from the principle of refusing any argument from authority. Concern for otherness, so strongly affirmed in contemporary philosophy, thus also tends to take the form of a "religion of the other." This sacralization of the human as such presupposes the move from what we could call a "vertical transcendence" (of things external to and higher than individuals, situated so to speak above them) to a "horizontal transcendence" (that of other human beings in relation to me).

To do justice to such a shift, it would be necessary to write a history of sacrifice. For what motives and what things have humans, over the course of time, given the gift of their own life, or at least some aspect of it? For sacrifice that is willingly consented to, whatever content we give it or whatever its scope, always implies, at least for anyone who believes it is urgently needed, the recognition of a meaning higher than our own existence. Such a person admits, whether explicitly or not, that a kind of beyond contains a greater value than does the here and now. The important moments of such a history might be, for example (although these examples are not chosen by chance): the greater glory of God, the nation, the revolution, following an order that runs from the more to the less vertical, from the divine to the human. For romanticism, the "people" tended to occupy the place formerly reserved for God. It constituted a higher entity than the mere sum of individuals who made it up. For all that, it did represent a certain humanization of the divine. The same thing goes for the revolution; it too is superior to the individuals who died for it, yet it is at the same time already inscribed within the earthly order.

Today, giving oneself for one's country or for some revolutionary cause is no longer on the menu. Has sacrifice then completely disappeared from our ethical horizon? I have already suggested that the answer is no. What is true is that it has profoundly changed its nature. If our fellow citizens are hardly predisposed to sacrifice themselves for "vertical" values, imposed from above like some external force, they do sometimes seem ready to do so for other beings, *provided that they are human beings.*

I am aware of how arbitrary such an affirmation may seem. The notion of "sacrifice" is an infinite source of misunderstandings. It has unfortunate theological connotations and is easily confused with some forms of mortification to which most ancient religions seem attached. Is it necessary to emphasize that by this term I do not mean that traditional understanding? I am thinking instead of the requirement of concern for the other so often asserted, if only in words, as an indispensable counterweight to concern for oneself alone. Aren't our societies more marked by hedonism, egoism, and cowardliness than by the sense of sacrifice? Don't they tolerate within themselves millions of excluded people and, at their very doors, the most iniquitous wars and massacres? Aren't they insensitive to the spectacle of "suffering at a distance" that countless televised images have served more to exorcise than to relieve? And isn't the little devotion we do observe, when not diverted to serve the media, mostly limited to the private sphere, more to the circle of those related to us than to our "neighbors," and by this very fact a part of individualism?

Without dwelling on the discussion these legitimate questions raise, I want merely to observe that the gift of oneself, even when it is limited to one's own children, remains highly enigmatic. Nor is it sure that it is confined today just to the sphere of those related to us. However fragile, however questionable it may be, humani-

tarian action bears witness to a new aspiration, one that is not to
be confused with the traditional forms of charity. Beyond the criticism that we can address to it *on the political level*, it makes manifest
the requirement for solidarity with humanity as a whole, a solidarity, therefore, *that is no longer bound to ancient communal ties,* whether
religious, ethnic, national, or familial. No doubt this aspiration is
still embryonic in practice. It is even possible that it can sometimes
provide an alibi for political inaction. Nevertheless, it does indicate
an ideal that makes manifest the move from a vertical to a horizontal transcendence, one in which it is human existence as such
that constitutes an immediate demand on my responsibility. And
it is on this specifically modern basis insofar as it intends the other
in general, not just someone to whom I have some preestablished
connection owing to tradition, that the question of the gift of oneself has to be reformulated.

We live not so much at the end of sacrificial values as, in the
proper sense, at the time of their humanization—the time of a
move from a religious conception of sacrifice to the idea that sacrifice is required only *by and for humanity itself.* It is this new task that
governs the appearance in the ethical order of hitherto unheard-
of preoccupations. Malraux's well-known comment about "the
possibility of a spiritual event on planetary scale" that will be the
mark of the twenty-first century is another impetus for our reflection, no doubt because the long process by which the divine with-
drew from our social and political universe turns out to be linked
to a divinization of humanity that redirects us toward new forms
of spirituality. I am not using this term here in a loose, uncontrolled
way, even though it may remain in one sense analogical, for where
there is sacrifice there is also the idea of higher values. And the
fact that they are today perceived as incarnate in humanity and
not in some vertical transcendence doesn't change a thing. Or
rather, it does. It changes the relation of human beings to the sacred but in no way implies its complete disappearance, up to and
including the collective order. The new transcendence is no less
imposing than the old one, even if it is imposing in another way. It
remains the demand for an order of meaning that, finding its root
in human beings, still refers to a radical exteriority. Previously situated as coming before ethics, which it claimed to ground, the sa-

cred today falls on the other side. And in this move from upstream to down, from theological ethics to the ethical-religious, lies the secret of moral systems yet to come.

It is in this sense, it seems to me, that the ethics of authenticity is in no way the last word on contemporary moral philosophy. After a period of protest during the sixties, when it claimed to revolutionize the structures of bourgeois morality, today it is confined to adding a corrective by pleading, sometimes with good reason, for a greater concern for the individual. But the will to realize a perfect self-immanence is a failure. And this is so for one basic reason, which we must now try to make clearer. The requirement of autonomy, so dear to modern humanism, does not suppress the notion of sacrifice, or that of transcendence. Simply, and this is what must be understood, it implies a *humanization of transcendence and, owing to this very fact, not the eradication but rather a displacement of the traditional figures of the sacred*. Love, previously reserved for the Divinity (or for higher entities than humans, like the fatherland or the revolution), has been humanized and, for the same reasons, the ideologies of sacrifice along with it. Without disappearing, they have been transformed and, above all, have changed their object. If we are willing to see in sacrifice one of the measures of the sacred, as the very etymology of the word invites us to do, we have to complement the history of religion and of ethics with that of the representation of human feelings. Taking this as a guideline will permit us to grasp how the adventures of the sacred have been perceived by the subjects who, in the end, are the only real heroes and how, in this very way, the question of the meaning of their life will bit by bit be reintegrated into the space of modern humanism.

The Birth of a Life of Feeling

Over the past few years, the historians of *mentalités* have forged one hypothesis of broad importance. Everything, in effect, indicates that over the centuries, and at least during the three centuries preceding the Enlightenment and the birth of the democratic universe (from the fifteen century to the eighteenth),[7] the governing principle of the family had practically no connection with what we ordinarily call "love." Beginning with the work of Ariès,[8] these researchers invite us to relativize our tendency to take as "natural"[9] what has come about historically. We know today that during the Middle Ages,[10] in Europe at least, the death of a spouse or a child was not always taken to be a catastrophe—not by a long shot. Broadly speaking, feeling was not the foundation of the traditional family. In order for affective affinity for others, rather than what tradition imposed, to constitute a new mode of family organization, it was necessary that modern subjectivity should come into existence and that the notion of a free individual should become a concrete sociological reality. It was only on this individualistic basis that people began to feel their mourning over the loss of a husband or wife, a son or daughter as a "heartfelt pain" that would allow them to draw from within themselves the resources for future sacrifices.[11]

The new history, that of Ariès in particular, gives us an insight into this decisive mutation in that it teaches us that in the classical age death was still (1) announced to the dying person, not concealed with white lies;[12] (2) public, not kept in the private sphere like a secret or an indiscretion; and (3) familiar and almost "tamed," whereas we find it abnormal and anxiety producing, as though it were due to an accident, when it is not a question of a temporary failure of modern medicine.[13] There is therefore a great distance between a death that, for the rich as for the poor, ordinarily took place in the presence of relatives, neighbors, and even passersby and a modern death that is more and more taken from the family and removed to the solitude of the hospital.

Let us consider for a moment this comparative indifference to the act of dying. More than consolation drawn from religion or from those around one, what seems to have led to the calmness of our ancestors was their implicit refusal of the modern notion of individuality thought of as one's being an atom, a monad cut off from one's ancestors and descendants by an *absolute* gap. For a long time people would respond to the question "Who are you?" by citing their lineage: "I am the son or daughter of . . . " This attitude made sense in the days when the idea of an individual, free in his choices and alone in his intimacy, was so to speak unknown. One defined oneself as a member of an indivisible line of descent. If there was any individuality, it lay more in the lineage itself than in this or that particular human being. The birth of the subject who was his own master, self-defined by his commitments and choices, implied on the contrary that he would cease thinking of himself first as one part of an organic whole.[14] As a result, death had to change its meaning and indifference had to give way to anxiety.[15] It took on the terrifying allure of a complete oblivion, so to speak, rather than just being one incident *of life itself.*

Hegel, and already before him the romantics, still affirmed this when they considered the relation of the species to those particular living beings composing it. The latter had to reproduce and die so that the universal life of the former could perpetuate itself. Today we continue to think of the death of animals in such a "holistic" way. We attach a price to it only depending on their degree of individualization. If the animal is a pet, humanized through our feelings for it, the pain is sometimes intense. If it is a wild animal and its species is not endangered, we consider its death a natural phenomenon that there is no reason for us to be particularly concerned about.

This latter remark, of course, has only a metaphorical value. I do not mean to suggest that people in the past considered their fellows as we do animals. However, the absence of individuation, owing to the weight of lineage and of community, does explain why these two could play, mutatis mutandis, a role analogous to that of the species in the dialectic of life described by Hegel. Just as universal life is superior to particular beings who die for it, lineage, tradition, and the weight of community were infinitely more important than the individual. The individual had to have been aware of this, to such an extent that, seeing himself as a part of some higher entity, he could relativize his own end. Traditional communitarianism must thus have reinforced faith so that the conviction would have prevailed that death was a transition, a mere change of state. The autonomous individual, cut off from what precedes and what follows him, can no longer allow himself such a luxury. Absolute for and through himself, to him death will appear like an absolute nothingness, and his religious beliefs, if he still possesses any, will no longer be built on ancient forms of solidarity. Whence the decisive breaks that Edward Shorter, in synthesizing the indubitable acquisitions of this new history, pinpoints between the modern family, progressively coming into place starting in the eighteenth century, and the traditional European family. They have to do with the nature of marriage, the birth of private life, and the advent of parental love. They all are associated with the intrusion of "feeling" into every family relationship as well as with the emancipation of individuals as opposed to the grip of earlier communitarian and religious traditions. The connection between these two major phenomena will contribute forcefully to shifting the idea of the sacred toward new objects, less external to human beings. It will also push, for the same reasons, toward a humanization of the motives for sacrifice.

Marriage Based on Love, the Birth of Private Life, and the Advent of Parental Affection

Contrary to an idea often put forth by traditionalists, the family did not disappear along with the Ancien Régime. It is even one of those rare institutions that has so endured beyond the revolution that today it finds itself full of life and probably, despite the high number of divorces, more stable than ever. However, this permanence must not conceal the depth of changes, even upheavals, that have occurred since the eighteenth century. The most important of them, undoubtedly, is the passage from a marriage of "convenience," in light of some economic end and most often organized by the parents or, through them, by the village community, to a marriage based on love, freely chosen by the partners themselves. Here is how one of our best historians, François Lebrun, describes this evolution:

> In comparison with today, the functions of the conjugal family of the past were essentially economic. A unit for consumption and production, it had also to ensure the preservation and transmission of a patrimony. The couple was formed from these economic bases through the choice and will of the parents or sometimes of the man and woman themselves, but without their feelings having much to do with it. . . . In such conditions, the family could only secondarily have affective and educative functions. A good marriage was one of conve-

nience, not one based on love. Of course, love might subsequently be born from life together, but a love filled with reserve, owing nothing to passionate love, which was left to extramarital relationships.[16]

For us, as heirs of the romantics, the principle of a union based on feelings almost goes without saying. The way we think of the couple has lost almost every signification that it still had during the classical age: to ensure the permanence of a lineage and of family property by the spouses' taking into account the necessities of production and reproduction. If we are so quick to deplore the very idea of a "marriage for money," it is certainly because we have forgotten the objectives of such an arrangement. We should recall that according to an edict of February 1556 against "clandestine marriages," children who married without their parents' permission were disinherited and declared to be outside the law. In 1579 an ordinance in Blois considered as abductors, to be sentenced to death "without hope of grace or pardon," those "minors" of less than twenty-five who might have married without their parents' consent![17] The idea of condemning to death those under twenty-five years old who married without the approval of their parents, as was the case in France during the sixteenth century, seems so archaic to us that we overlook the fact that the men and women of the time saw good reasons for this.

No doubt the most widely held opinion of our own time, perhaps the only one to attain unanimity, is that life in common is a matter of one's own feelings and choice. It stems from individual *private* decisions—that is, from decisions removed as far as possible from the grip of the surrounding society. It is even in the name of this "sentimental" vision of human relationships that marriage, even marriage based on love, sometimes gets called into question. It still owes too much to traditions; it is an unneeded concession to the community that genuine feelings ought to do without.

Whence the second break, which all the historians of the family agree in emphasizing: in past times intimacy did not exist, either among the common people or among the elite. In the city as in the countryside, the vast majority of families lived in a single room,[18] something that de facto excluded the possibility of any form of *pri-*

vacy. What suggests that such privacy was not yet an object of desire was that it did not as yet exist among the bourgeoisie or the aristocracy, even when their economic resources made it possible.[19] Ariès has shown, through his analyses of the architecture of the grand bourgeois or noble houses, that the rooms, although numerous, had no special function and generally opened onto one another with a lack of discrimination that would seem unbearable to us today. It was only in the eighteenth century that there came into being corridors meant to ensure autonomy and to isolate different spaces.

Another face of this nonrecognition of the private sphere is that the community felt free to intervene in family life in a way that seems inconceivable to us. Testifying to this, among other signs, was the practice of the "charivari" that historians of the family have found it important to study. It is significant that this odd and noisy ceremony by which a community expressed its disapproval of a deviant couple was aimed above all at cuckolded or battered husbands. Because of their weakness or inability to establish their authority as head of the family, they placed the community in danger. The community had therefore to signal a call to order in a domain where one can understand that this was not yet considered a strictly private affair. Some regions associated the charivari with the *azouade*, where the unhappy husband was led across the village seated backward on an ass. Jean-Louis Flandrin emphasizes as one symptom of the exorbitant weight of the community in family affairs that in the absence of the husband (who might have fled) the nearest neighbor was tied to the ass, to remind him of his duty of surveillance, hence his indirect responsibility for the misbehavior of his fellow citizens!

The third break, the one constituted by the advent of parental love, is not, one must think, unrelated to the other two. Isn't marriage based on love, chosen by the individuals involved and not imposed on them by tradition, one of the most likely conditions for feeling affection toward one's children? Undoubtedly it would be incorrect or excessive to claim that the maternal "instinct" or love did not exist. Undoubtedly parents have always felt a minimum of attachment for their progeny, if only in the natural, biological form we observe among most animal species. However, one of the most astonishing conclusions of recent historical study is that parental love was far from being a priority, as it has become for most couples today. Far from it for many people, as the following simple, well-known anecdote testifies in a way strongly indicative of an attitude that would evolve slowly from the sixteenth century to the eighteenth. Montaigne, the great humanist, admitted not remembering exactly how many of his children had died while given over to wet nurses! This says much about the abyss that separates us from the Renaissance. This is surely all the more true in that this ignorance was not due to some hardness of heart on the part of the philosopher. His attitude stands instead as one symptom of a dominant form of behavior during his day toward those still "potential" beings who were children.[20]

From an analogous perspective, the notion of parents' "duties" toward their progeny did not seem to impose itself on society as a whole until the beginning of the eighteenth century (in quite varying degrees depending on social level). Essentially, the relation was the reverse in the classical age. As Jean-Louis Flandrin shows,

> In the seventeenth century, it was still thought that the child owed everything to his father because he owed him life. "If both the one and the other find themselves in the same necessity, the son should give help to his father rather than to his own son," Fernandès de Moure considered, "inasmuch as he has received a greater good from his parents than from his children." That a father could sacrifice himself for his children was one of the paradoxes of Christianity, and in the seventeenth century the sacrifice of Christ still had this paradoxical character. "Fathers give life to their children, and this is without any doubt a great favour," exclaimed Father Cheminais in the second half of the century, "but one has never seen a father who has preserved the life of his children with his own blood, and who has died so that they might live, as did our Heavenly Father."[21]

"One has never seen a father who . . ." is undoubtedly an affirmation whose goal is to underscore the exceptional and admirable character of the sacrifice Christ consented to. But to have an effect, the argument must have found some echo among those who heard it. This is corroborated by the study of catechisms and confessional manuals that appeared from the fourteenth century to the eighteenth. Until the middle of the sixteenth century, they all dwell at length on children's duties toward their parents and almost never the opposite. It is only quite cautiously, step by step, that this idea appears beginning toward the end of the sixteenth century, only to blossom during the eighteenth. The contrast is striking, and Flandrin explains its origin in this way:

> Among the social élites at this time, a number of heads of families were bent on achieving the ascent of their house, and an excessively numerous family threatened to wreck this ambition. . . . In these families, the child who embodied the hopes of social ascent of the father was cherished. On the other hand, when a dozen other children arrived who could prevent the father rounding off his fortune and would filch from the heir a part of the patrimony, thus imperiling the rise of the family, it is understandable that he should have taken a dislike to them. Speaking in more general terms, the inability to control births multiplied the unwanted children. And the hope of getting rid of them by death might suggest itself all the more easily to some minds because infant mortality was, as is known, considerable, especially among children from towns put out to nurse in the country. It may well not have been not without malign intent that, in many bourgeois families, the mother nursed the heir, and the other children were put out to nurses.[22]

This frightening suspicion seems all the more justified in that the use of a wet nurse, which it is estimated affected between one-fifth and one-sixth of the babies during the eighteenth century,[23] not to speak of infanticide pure and simple, often amounted to a sentence of death. And it seems that the parents were not unaware of this fact.[24] The statistics are striking. In the second half of the eighteenth century between 62 and 75 percent of the children given to a wet nurse died before reaching one year old! These "dead infants" did not seem to upset either their parents or society or the mercenary wet nurses. Flandrin reports the case of one wet nurse who, over the course of twenty years, had had a dozen children entrusted to her but did not give one back alive; yet this fact seems not to have upset anyone! We also know that the horrible practice of swaddling was still in force. It was not just a form of torture for the nursing children, it also placed their health and life in danger. As for abandonment, even an author as concerned to reevaluate the past as the American historian John Boswell estimates, in drawing on recent research, that it must have risen, even as late as the eighteenth century, to almost 30 percent of the registered births![25] This was a sad fate, since in Paris, for which we have trustworthy figures, the children taken in by the Hospital had no more than one chance in ten of reaching the age of ten years because the death rate due to illness, but also to indifference and poor treatment, was so high.[26] François Lebrun reports as wholly genuine and in conformity with reality the following description of the conditions under which abandoned infants from the provinces were brought to the great hospital in Paris.

> A man carried the newborn infants on his back in a padded chest that could hold three of them. They were upright in their shirts, breathing air that came in through the top. The man stopped only to eat and to give them a bit of milk. When he opened his box, he often found one of them dead. He finished his trip with the two others, impatient to get rid of them at the drop-off place. When he had deposited them at the hospital, he returned to the country to recommence his work, which was his way of earning a living.[27]

Here is one last figure, which will not be surprising after what has preceded it: it is estimated that 90 percent of the infants died, either as a direct result of this trip or within three months after their admission, and neither society nor the communal conscience was particularly offended by this!

How could love and affection come to take the place of such traditional bonds and indifference? For what reasons did such a revolution in attitude become the rule? Despite their diversity, the interpretations that have been given converge on what was essential. It was owing to the passage from a holistic, hierarchical society to an individualistic and egalitarian one that the influence of affection in personal relations could increase. In this regard,

Shorter offers an insight that has the merit of clearness. With the birth of capitalism and salaried work, men and women found themselves constrained, at least in the labor market, to act as *self-determining* individuals, challenged as they were to pursue their own ends and particular interests. And these new imperatives led, in a quite concrete manner, to the obligation to leave older communities one belonged to—for the peasants, for example, to "move to the city," something that conferred on them a slight margin of freedom in relation to the weight of traditional customs. In substance, Shorter's thesis is that the individualistic reflexes and push toward freedom were not equally shared. Acquired in the sphere of the market, they were bit by bit transposed to those of culture and human relations. In all these domains, in effect, the weight of the community diminished to the same degree that free individual decision making increased. How could those who chose their work not come to want the right to choose their female or male companions?[28] Thus the logic of individualism as it was introduced into human relationships elevated them to the sphere of modern, elective love based on emotion.

In this way the question of the meaning of life found itself inverted. Henceforth it will be secular love that gives the most significance to individual existence. It is what will best incarnate the "personal structure of meaning." We might be tempted to see in it a promise of emancipation and happiness. Yet all of modern literature, with an insistence that is striking, invariably describes it in terms of unhappiness. From *The Princess of Cleves* to *The Sentimental Education*, from *The Charterhouse of Parma* to *Belle du Seigneur*, the same warning constantly reappears. There is no such thing as happy love. It is as though the site of meaning is cursed, as though the happiness it promises is by nature doomed to failure. I have already suggested that this love involves a certain imprudence, bound as it immediately is to the strongest but also the most changing attachments. From this point of view, to be sure, the psychology of the passions, assisted by psychoanalysis or not, does not lack explanations for what seems to be our fate. But these reasons, however apt they may be, perhaps do not reach what is essential. Indeed, it may be for properly metaphysical reasons that the emotional life of modern people runs into greater difficulties than those detected by anthropology. I see at least two such reasons this should be so.

The Tragic Aspect of Modern Love

The first such reason follows quite directly from what has already been said: individuals are henceforth required to found the most important part of their existence on their feelings, on sometimes violent emotional attachments, even as they find themselves more than ever deprived of the aid of traditions—of religious belief, but also of the support provided by a community based on a concrete experience of solidarity. This is a tragic circle, since the two movements—the rise of feeling as well as the withdrawal of traditions—multiply each other's effects. Bad things become more deeply felt at the same time as they make less sense. It is a risky life, and attempts to renew older forms of spirituality thrive on denouncing it. They go out of their way to point out the flagrant contradictions of a mortal existence that organizes its own unhappiness in advance by cultivating attachments apart from any meditation on separation or death. In this we can see the scope of the difficulties modern people must be prepared to face: more love and emotional ties than ever toward those near one, more vulnerability to unhappiness and evil in every form, but less support than ever in the face of it. I say this not to denounce "modernity" but rather to underscore one of the high prices we must pay for its individualistic ideal. Whence, also, without a doubt, the continued resurgence of antimodern and neotraditional ideologies. From deep ecology to different forms of New Age thinking, passing through the various forms of religious syncretism so much in vogue today, these all call for a return to forms of communitarian, not to say sectarian, spirituality. Whence too their difficulty in being convincing over the long term in a universe where their disciples themselves, caught up in the general movement of the age, despite their holistic convictions, never stop laying claim to the individualistic values of authenticity and of "thinking for yourself," up to choosing your own guru!

But there is a second, less trivial and less visible, reason for the threats that weigh on emotional happiness. Once freed from those sacred bonds imposed by religious and communitarian traditions, individuals have to confront a hitherto unknown type of human relations—the face-to-face relationship, the duality (or should I say solitariness?) of a couple now handed over to itself, freed from the weight of the vertical world of tradition but also deprived of its aid. A human, all too human couple perhaps that is going to experience the close relationship uniting absolute freedom and the fragility of happiness.[29]

The Dialectic of Our Love Life: Tristan, Don Juan, and Back Again

Are the feelings that give rise to passion sufficient to found enduring relationships? Aren't they by nature so unstable that nothing solid can be built on them?[30] This has been felt all the way back to Plato, and nothing today has refuted it. Yet modern people believe that without a love life, emotions are not worth having. Such is the paradox of marriage based on love. It seems to bear within itself from its very outset, almost essentially, its own dissolution. If feeling alone joins two beings, it alone can also disunite them.[31] The more marriage breaks free from traditional, economic, or family reasons to become based on individual choice and elective affinity, the more it runs into the typically modern question of the "wearing out" of desire. It is as though love, having only one lifetime, must bring every union to its breakup.

Drewermann suggests that this fall is just the effect of another, older one.[32] It was not the mere fact of the sins of the flesh that drove Adam and Eve from paradise, but rather their separation from a transcendence that permitted their relationship. The loss of a third term, the divine, gave them over to each other, to a face-to-face relationship doomed sooner or later to destruction. For once Drewermann cannot be suspected of proposing an original or deviant interpretation. On the contrary, what he says is fully in harmony with the best-attested orthodoxy when he rediscovers the genuine sense of *temptation*. It is the work par excellence of the serpent, of that *diabolos* who aims at a separation from the divine as such and who takes great pleasure in the devastating effects this produces on humankind.

For centuries, in Christian Europe, the only love that was held to be legitimate was reserved for God. The Gospels even insist on this with a rigor that many Christians today are no longer capable of hearing. "Whoever comes to me and does not hate father and mother, wife and children, brothers and sisters, yes, and even life itself, cannot be my disciple" (Luke 14:26). Undoubtedly shocked by the force of the verb "hate" or its unexpected appearance in a message supposedly entirely animated by love, some translators have sought to replace it with other words, which seem less brutal to them.[33] But this is to gloss over the meaning of what is said. It is not, to be sure, that Christ preaches hate per se for one's relatives.[34] But *merely* human love does seem detestable to him, and it is this exclusive emphasis that he invites us to hate. Without the mediation of a transcendence, or a third term that unites things, it is doomed to be nothing. But it is this third term, we understand, that the birth of individualism has taken from us. The modern family is in the first place and above all else a *couple* to whom may be attached, as the case may be, but unlike in the past not out of any necessity, "relatives" in the broad sense found in American English, which thereby designates, without thinking about it, the new face of the absolute.

Whether or not one is a believer, it is difficult to be totally un-aware of the warning here. It does a good job of explaining the ruses that passion makes use of when, finally freed of all religious "illusions," it throws itself into a frantic search for the obstacles that make possible or retard its metamorphoses. We shall spare ourselves here the need to list them, assuming they are well known to everyone. For at least two centuries now, these strategies have provided the most obvious target of an immense literature. Still, it is interesting, before any talk about the hypothesis that these twists and turns are the substitute for some lost transcendence, to think about the visible effects of a dialectic that two monads find them-selves caught up in for better or worse—the dialectic of egoism and altruism. It runs through and nourishes the whole modern issue of passionate love. Novelists, commentators, even serious phi-losophers have asked the question: Isn't this form of love contradic-tory? On the one hand, the lover says he (she) is totally absorbed by his (her) object. He (she) is, so to speak, totally "outside" himself (herself). He (she) thinks only of her (him), sees only her (him) in his (her) dreams, and every instant is attentive to the slightest sign coming from the other person. He (she) is, if you will, an "altruist." But are these emotions really one's own? Where are those passionate feelings situated if not in one's own heart of hearts? Is not the object, who a moment ago seemed so essential, not in truth the accessory, the contingent cause of an affect that by nature is egoistic and that above all feeds on itself?

Of course it is impossible to decide between these two possibilities. Yet this argument, which seems so theoretical, takes on a quite concrete import through the unfolding of one's love life. Passion, if it is to survive, needs a perfect equality between lover and beloved. Everyone, apart from a few innocents, feels this. In love, any disequilibrium is fatal. This axiom, while a fundamental law of physics, is no less that of the heart and as such is no less constraining than that of the body. Simone Weil, as is well known, made it the central theme of a small book whose opening words are eloquent. "All the natural movements of the soul are controlled by laws analogous to those of physical gravity. Grace is the only exception. . . . What is the reason that as soon as one human being shows he needs another (no matter whether his need be slight or great) the latter draws back from him? Gravity." [35] And if this disequilibrium is fatal, isn't it because individuals handed over to the solitude of the face-to-face relationship can only vacillate between these two extremes that are the annihilation of the self to the "profit" (but what a pitiful profit) of the other and the annihilation of the other to the profit of the self?

Undoubtedly readers will find this assertion excessive, and they will be right. Sometimes, it is true, passionate love does find an equilibrium. Then it is transformed into a happy and caring friendship. In short, it ages well. But this is because it has ceased to be a passion and allows the individuals involved to exit that solitude of two people by themselves to make a place for other things that both separate them and bind them together as monads. It is passion that is excessive, not the things we say about it. It is what, as the most truthful clichés have it, "devours" us. It is no accident, in this sense, that our great erotic myths, from Tristan to Don Juan, are so antithetical, that they are inscribed within the circle of a dialectic where the figures of altruism and egoism stand opposed to each other like the terms of an antinomy. And if they have taken on this symbolic force, isn't it also because these two extremes, which constantly point back to each other, define the contours of the emotional space proper to individualism?

The Suitor: Self-Negation to the Profit of Another

Being unable to preserve a perfect equilibrium, the ideal reciprocity of feelings, over the long haul, passionate love takes refuge in a self-negation that comes down to a kind of mysticism. Just as the mystic seeks a "fusion with God," lovers seek to disappear into the beloved. All that is left is a sigh, but at least they have at their disposal a well-tested model, that of courtly love, already apparent in the poetry of the twelfth century, then reinterpreted by the romantics for use by modern people.[36] The idealization of the loved one is its principal motif. The beloved's perfection—a qualification ordinarily reserved for the divine—is what unleashes intense feelings, imprinting them in the lover's heart like a stamp applied to wax. Here passion takes on its true meaning—that of absolute passivity. Just as sensation, from a "realistic" perspective, is caused by the impact of the world created by God on a passive sensibility, feelings are the effect necessarily produced by the shock of the encounter with the loved one.[37] Courtly love is therefore by nature unhappy. The beloved must always remain transcendent—which is why the relation most often remains platonic, both disinterested and disembodied. It is through self-negation that the suitor attempts to remove the gap engendered by the disequilibrium of terms. In wholly abolishing himself, he can hope to reestablish a connection to that quasi-divine being that is the object of his love. It is only through death that Tristan finally raises himself to the level of a union for which no terrestrial incarnation is in truth possible.

With this we can also see how this ideal abnegation, this hyperbolic "altruism," can easily invert itself into the contrary: narcissism. Doesn't the idealization of the loved one, which is situated at the edge of idolatry, stem from what we today would call "projection"? This process becomes flagrant in its reappropriation by the romantics, particularly in Stendhal, when he describes the phenomenon of "crystallization."[38] By leaving behind its religious motifs (the idealization of a metaphysical perfection, fusion with the perfect being through self-negation), passionate love dooms the lover, who wants to annihilate himself in the beloved, to finding himself alone with himself. First of all, this is thanks to the law of the "weight of things," such as the unfortunate Stendhal so cruelly experienced with Mathilde Dembowski. But it is also because idealization, quickly reduced to projection, only ever leads back to the interior life of the lover. He sinks into that easy complacency toward himself that is the love of love, even unhappy love. Setting aside the rhetoric of negating the ego in favor of the other, the suitor is nothing more than the laughable hero of a solitary egoism.

The Myth of Don Juan: The Negation of the Other to the Profit of the Ego

The beloved then becomes something different. To be, in truth, is to perceive or to be perceived, to love or to be loved. Don Juan is the emotional equivalent of this idealist theory of perception. He constantly seduces, but the objects of his charms have only an indistinguishable existence. Women for him are merely silhouettes, and it is through this negation of the other that he affirms his supreme power and his freedom. One can no more imagine Don Juan married than Tristan, but the reasons for this impossibility are reversed. The perfect being was inaccessible to the suitor, so the lover, renouncing the beloved, falls into nothingness. Now he is the one who is inaccessible, he is the one who is the whole of reality, and its interchangeable objects become unreal. So Don Juan speaks of his conquests as of some confused, sexless mass: "Whatever happens, I cannot refuse my heart *to anything that I see as lovable.*"[39] The only thing that counts in his eyes are his subjective "experiences," not the particular beings who are their contingent cause. As a strict egoist, it is by way of them that he hopes to grasp himself, to finally coincide with himself in the enjoyment of vital energies that procure constant renewals for him. "Newborn inclinations, after all, have an inexplicable charm, and the whole pleasure of love is in change."[40]

This absolute freedom, that means to rule alone over many

hearts, also inverts itself into its contrary. Even when he intends to experience himself, Don Juan is doomed never to grasp himself except through a perpetual exteriority. He wants to incarnate the most perfect egoism, but he constantly has to appeal to the otherness of another, one who is indeterminate, yes, but nevertheless essential to his life. Developing the worship of the new for its own sake, he is led back to the abstract repetition of moments of existence that, although not without charm at their origin, all end up resembling one another. Excitement gives way to boredom, pure difference to the sad identity of a night where all cats are gray.

In this way the dialectic brings us back, as it must, to its starting point. Unable to maintain the equilibrium of its terms, the amorous consciousness seeks in vain to preserve their unity by negating one of them. According to Kierkegaard, this is the supreme failing of the "aesthetic stage." As a good Christian, he concludes that the love between two beings must be joined with a third that at the same time both transcends and unifies them. Our hypothesis can thus find a translation in terms of the framework of a certain kind of humanism, one that finally accepts considering the transcendence of the other as compatible with self-immanence—as what, starting from inside the ego and its feelings, breaks through the overly narrow bounds of the individual monad.

The New Faces of Love

At this stage of our reflections, it is time to examine a question that no doubt has already occurred to many readers. When one talks of the "birth of modern love," as I have done here by basing myself on the results of the history of *mentalités,* just what love is one talking about? Who can say that men and women of the past did not love one another just as we do today? Was it really necessary to wait for the Enlightenment for Christianity to preach love? Clearly not. But just as clearly, the term is equivocal. It covers many different realities. Hence it will help to make things more precise. Let us start from the old so we can better grasp what is new, for us, from ancient Hellenism. It is widely known that Greek made use of three words for love: *eros, philia,* and *agape.*[41]

As for *eros,* it is undoubtedly Plato who tells us what is essential.

Freud, twenty-three centuries later, only repeats what he has to say: sexual desire, caught up in loving passion, is really a lack. It calls for *consummation* from the other. Once satisfied, it loses itself in the nothingness of sleep until it reawakens and starts over again with no other ultimate end than death itself. The German word Freud uses to designate *eros* contains this contradiction in itself, which is that of all biological life: *Lust,* meaning both desire and pleasure, lack and satisfaction, because they cannot exist without each other. All "excitement" tends toward its own suppression, which is why *eros* always gives way to *thanatos,* death.

For *philia,* usually translated as friendship, we have to turn instead to Aristotle. He has devoted to it the finest pages in his *Nicomachean Ethics.* Unlike *eros, philia* does not live on lack and consummation, but on the contrary exists in that precious, singular joy that is born from the simple presence, the mere existence, of the beloved.[42] Everyone can think of some concrete reality for which these definitions take on a greater precision. It is in this sense of *philia* that historians teach us how much it was lacking in the traditional family, to the point of constituting, at least within the framework of European civilization, a real revolution with its appearance during the eighteenth century.

What then of *agape?* Not found in Greek antiquity, it appears in the Gospels to indicate the love that Christ tells us to extend toward those who are indifferent to us, and even to our enemies. A love, therefore, that does not feed on some lack in the other (*eros*) any more than it rejoices in his presence (*philia*) but instead, in a way difficult for humans to envisage, finds its model in Christ's crucifixion—a disinterested, gratuitous, even unjustified love, since it clearly continues to act apart from any reciprocity. One of the rare images we can form of it is undoubtedly the love of a mother (or father) for an ill-behaved son (or daughter) that she (he) nonetheless continues to cherish. Or again this one, even rarer, which Comte-Sponville refers to, inspired by Simone Weil: not always to take all the available space but to allow the other whom one loves to exist.[43] "You take a step back? He takes two. Simply to leave you more room, not to crowd you in, not to invade your space. . . . This is the contrary of what Sartre called 'the big so and so, so full of being,' in which he saw the plausible definition of a dirty rotten bastard. If we accept his definition, which implies another one, we have to say that charity, insofar as we are capable of it, would be the contrary of this ugly, nasty way of being oneself. It would be something like a renunciation of the fullness of being an ego, of strength, of power."[44] These are, of course, only approximations, but they do tend, we sometimes say, to give us an idea, or rather a sensible outline, of what perhaps no longer belongs wholly to the sphere of human feelings.

André Comte-Sponville draws a lesson from his consideration of these three forms of love that is worth thinking further about. It is clear that in the sense of *philia* I can never love more than ten to twenty people in this world. But there are plenty more, more than five billion in fact, who fall outside the field of this kind of love. Beyond *philia*, as a result, the realm of morality, of legal, abstract, and in truth indifferent respect takes over. It is what allows me to act almost as though I loved those whose lack hardly matters to me and whose existence is a matter of indifference. It is what orders me to write a check to help the homeless, to take part in a demonstration against some injustice, or more simply, to accept the idea that my freedom stops where others' begins. In short, a minimum of *consideration* that most of the time, if things go well, takes the place for us of *agape*. *Agape* would make morality superfluous, yet this kind of love is so gratuitous, so disinterested that it seems almost inaccessible to human beings, which is why the superfluous—that is, morality—becomes so necessary in the final analysis. "Act as though you loved": all things considered, this is the last word. It may not be much from the perspective of the ideal of Christ, but it is already a lot and even something heaven-sent if we think in terms of the facts of the world, such as they are.

To this analysis I would add only the following. If it is *philia* that gets taken into the family with the advent of modern individualism, is it so absurd to imagine that it makes us more open to the virtues of *agape?* Someone may object that love is egoistic, that the family, as the sphere of the private par excellence, does not concern itself with the collective except in response to the influences that the collective exercises on it. Parents worry about the economic situation when it poses a threat to their children, about school or the university when they enter it, about the future of medicine and social security when they are ill, and so on. None of this is untrue. Yet between this egoism of a few, on the one side, and the abstract morality of universalized imperatives on the other there is, it seems to me, an intermediary link, a noticeable hyphen that becomes really perceptible only following and through the intrusion of *philia* into the private realm. Even if we are first concerned about those close to us, we nonetheless feel some compassion in the face of the suffering of others whom we now know as alter egos. And this further requires that democratic equality be established along with the appearing of our modern emotional life. Without this mediation, no compassion would be possible toward humanity as a whole. And it seems to me that it is this actual *sympathy* that will lead to relativizing the narrow limits of an antinomy, that of egoism and altruism, that modern love first finds itself ensnared in. Such sympathy was necessary if the morality of duty was not to remain a pure abstraction, for it to have been, so to speak, made fruitful by *agape*. It is impossible for those who love their children to remain insensible to the misfortune that strikes those *like them*, even if they are on the other side of the world. Within a democratic framework where the idea that there is no natural difference between individuals takes its course, egoism is destined, *to however small a degree*, to surpass itself—if I may put it this way—through itself. Often this surpassing even has no need of reasoning or rational calculation. It was on this new basis that the humanitarian adventure was to arise during the nineteenth century. Thanks to it, humanitarianism could take over from a Christian religion whose traditional structure—that of a theological ethics—was literally undercut by the progress of individualism.

New Figures of the Sacred?

What historians have to teach us is most valuable. It allows us to better comprehend the impulses behind a history of sacrifice and, in this way, the representations human beings have made of the sacred. The slow process of the disenchantment of the world by means of which the humanization of the divine has come about thus turns out to have been compensated for by a parallel movement of the divinization of the human. And this makes highly problematic any diagnosis according to which we purely and simply have to deal with an erosion of transcendence *in any and all of its forms,* defeated by the effects of an implacable process—that of democratic individualism. On the contrary, everything indicates that these forms of transcendence are reconstituting themselves, first in the sphere of individual feeling and emotion, but also, without a doubt, well beyond it, by taking into consideration the whole of humanity. They may be experienced as immanent to individual subjects, but they also define a new space of the sacred. Next we have to measure the contours of this space.

CHAPTER THREE

The Sacred with a Human Face

The sixties were years of the emancipation of the body. For more than twenty centuries, the Judeo-Christian tradition had opposed the conceptual world to the sensory world, the beauty of ideas to the ugliness of instincts, spirit to matter, the soul to the body. A process of rehabilitation was needed. Marx, Nietzsche, and Freud, called to the witness box, were to help the oppressed open the way to a joyful, playful, unconstrained materialism. At the end of this struggle appeared sexual liberation and, in its wake, the first laws regarding abortion. Beneath its immoralist exterior, this revolt in truth meant itself to be more moral than the moth-eaten older bourgeois ethics. It pleaded for the emancipation of humanity as a whole.

But the world turned: the demand for absolute freedom ran into new obstacles. Today it is no longer so much a question of liberating our bodies as of preserving them from the eventual harm stemming from the accumulated strength of science, industry, and commerce. Are these real threats or only fantasies? The question is well worth asking. At least it is certain that following the time of emancipation has come the time of providing sanctuary, for the sacralization of a human body that must not be handed over with no means of protection to the powers of technoscience. As symbols of these new preoccupations, it was during the eighties that we saw the formation of commissions on ethics that were charged with evaluating the consequences of scientific progress.

It was during this same period, and for analogous reasons, that humanitarianism too came to the first rank of our moral preoccupations. Here again the contrast with the sixties is striking. It is not saying much to recall that in May 1968, during the days when everything was "political," charity had a bad press. Ridiculed by the philosophers of suspicion, it was cast, like the religion that most often inspired it, as the opium of the people. It was not from something charitable that the much-expected revolution was supposed to come. On the contrary, charity constituted the most obvious pitfall, the most formidable obstacle, the honey meant to conceal the bitter potion whose only purpose was to serve a genuine militancy—one that arrived by way of revolt, then by the political reconquest of a depraved state caught up in class interests.[1] Marxist and Nietzschean critiques of "pity" constituted an obligatory passage for the study of philosophy.[2] I myself recall the dazzling commentary of one professor who invited us to consider the revolutionary potentialities of this passage from *The Will to Power* devoted to Christian charity:

> This universal love of men is in practice the *preference* for the suffering, underprivileged, degenerate. . . . The species requires that the ill-constituted, weak, degenerate, perish: but it was precisely to them that Christianity turned as a conserving force; it further enhanced that instinct in the weak, already so powerful, to take care of and preserve themselves and to sustain one another. What is "virtue" and "charity" in Christianity if not just this mutual preservation, this solidarity of the weak, this hampering of selection?[3]

The proletarians were called on to become the new masters, and the masses that had become bourgeois, conservative, and sheeplike were the contemporary equivalent of these weak Christians.

No doubt this opposing of politics and humanitarianism has not disappeared. The suspicion that the latter may serve as an alibi for the former is even at the heart of many contemporary debates. The question is a real one. Yet here once again the situation has reversed itself. Over the past twenty-five years the number of non-government organizations with a charitable purpose has multiplied a hundredfold, while the last revolutionary militants have been relegated to the museum as examples of an extinct species. Whether or not one deplores this, it is no longer politics that presents the idea of a utopia, but rather the project of finally taking in hand the suffering and dignity of the other. And if humanitarianism does give rise to some hostile reactions, it is not because of its objectives, but rather because people sometimes suspect it of squandering a good idea for ideological or media ends.[4] Thus to the sacralization of the body corresponds one of the heart, and the values of charity—secularized, then rebaptized—benefit from an unexpected impetus. In words, someone may reply, but is it so in fact?

The bad is not always what is most certain. An important study on benevolent giving commissioned by the Fondation de France and conducted by Edith Archambault and Judith Boumendil, two scientists from the Centre Nationale pour Recherche Scientifique, appeared in April 1995. It made little impact.[5] Yet its conclusions, which are important, testify to a not negligible tendency toward such a "concern for the other," which many people have thought was merely a superficial fad. Any interpretation of the phenomenon is not self-evident, to be sure, and it would be too hasty to celebrate our contemporaries' turning into angels without other supporting evidence. Still, the facts it reports are impressive. More than 50 percent of French people in 1994 made some kind of donation (against 40 percent in 1993), with the total reaching 14.3 billion francs; in other words, a growth of 50 percent over 1990. When we add that a quarter of these donors were people not subject to income taxes, we can perhaps also exclude the pessimistic hypothesis that these manifestations we would have a priori to consider as a form of generosity were motivated by the economic calculation of a tax deduction. This is all the more true in that the charitable impulse is not limited to the simple check by which some think others are trying to buy a clean conscience. Indeed, during the same period volunteer work, in all its forms, added a million new participants who paid, we can say, with their persons! In 1975 Secours Catholique had 25,000 volunteers, in 1984 it had 52,000, in 1989 it had 66,000! International humanitarian acts, among all the different ways this charitable impulse gets divided, did not come first. They even came behind sporting clubs and health and social services. Yet they do occupy a symbolic place, to the point that they tend to stand for the whole phenomenon. This is misleading, yes, but not wholly unfounded. For solidarity today seeks to be universal. Assisted by a taste for adventure, it would like to move beyond its older national, ethnic, and religious boundaries. The nation, race, even the divine no longer appear as sacred as the suffering or the human dignity of everyone in common. Here we have something that is novel, perhaps, and that we need to think more deeply about, for this sacralization has many facets.

Bioethics: The Sacralization of the Human Body

In vitro fertilization, an abortion pill, artificial insemination, cloning, experiments on the human embryo, eugenics, new definitions of the limits of life and death, organ donations, genetic manipulation and therapies, predictive medicine—the press constantly reports on the unavoidable existential, ethical, and legal scenarios into which our new powers over ourselves have plunged us. Never before, perhaps, have traditional barriers been so put to the test. Never before, without a doubt, has the progress of science and technology given rise to questions with such broad moral and, let us dare to use the word, *metaphysical* implications. It is as though the sense of the sacred remains, in spite of the "death of God," but without our being given the spirituality or wisdom that should correspond to it. Three fundamental reasons today make it clear why the mixture of uneasiness and fascination coming from bioethics is not so distant from the theological theme of profanation.

They have to do first of all with the question of identity or of what makes us human. It not only is possible to preserve frozen embryos indefinitely and to implant them at will, thereby overturning the old intangible logic of the generations—a woman, for example, could become the mother of her sister[6]—we can also "clone" human beings, modify their stem cells, possibly causing mutations in our species. What is implicitly posed, therefore, is nothing less than the question of what it is that constitutes humanity as such and that we ought never to tamper with.

That these powers are entirely at our disposal in itself constitutes a problem. Not only do we, so to speak, find ourselves both judge and judged, but we cannot control, at least not yet, all the possible effects of such interventions in our own "nature." Hence contemporary science gives new life to the myths of Frankenstein's monster and the sorcerer's apprentice. The creatures we can produce run the risk of escaping us in an irremediable manner. The right to err is therefore forbidden us, and it turns out there is no experiment that can claim a special innocence.

This is why it seems to me we cannot fail to consider a third question, which is by no means small. By whom, following what procedures, and in the name of what explicit or implicit criteria can limits be imposed on the inevitable unfolding of individual demands, or even, as some would wish, on the very development of scientific research? Handed over to a destiny that we can henceforth construct, left alone with our own demons, we human beings will have to find within ourselves the answers to these questions. We shall have to *invent*, so to speak ex nihilo, rules of conduct in the face of the powers we have unleashed, while no one yet knows if we shall be able to control them.

These, I believe, are the kinds of moral preoccupations that we bring together under the heading "bioethics." And far from eradicating the sense of the sacred, the secularization of the world that accompanies the evolution of science makes it ever more tangible, because it shifts this sense of the sacred toward human beings and incarnates it in them. The human body, like Christ's, becomes a temple. Yet the divinity that dwells therein seems undiscoverable. It refers to a soul that we cannot name, even if some intuition of it remains. Following the Hegelian prophecy, the divine has left heaven to become immanent. Confronted with the possibility of cloning or genetic manipulations that may transform the human species for good, the atheist is no less fearful than the believer. It is just that, ever since the advent of man made god, this fear is no longer bound to some representation of commandments imposed by the Creator. Only the gravity of the questions posed still invokes this, like the photographic negative of a concern to which secular humanism has not been able to do justice. It is tied to respect for the creature per se, whose body takes on value only as a function of the heart within it. From the birth of modern love to the sacralization of humankind, this connection becomes ever more visible.

Humanitarianism or the Sacralization of the Heart

When Henry Dunant, with the help of Gustave Moynier, founded the Red Cross on 29 October 1863, he had only one idea in mind: to make the largest possible number of states finally acknowledge the "neutrality" that had been so dear to him ever since his first encounter with the ignominy of war. Others have already recounted the lofty and tumultuous story of what happened to Henry Dunant.[7] Here it is enough simply to mention the founding event, the primeval scene if you will, that provided the initial impulse—the well-known episode of Solferino. A fervent Protestant and a member of the established bourgeoisie in Geneva, Dunant sought adventure and fortune in Algeria, where he bought a modern, operating mill. However, the earth was not productive, and the authorities harassed him in innumerable ways, so he decided to appeal to the emperor. But in 1859 Napoleon III was not in Paris; he was in Italy, leading a ferocious war against the Austrians. Dunant was confident. So he went to Lombardy to confront him. On 24 June his carriage stopped at Castiglione, a few kilometers from the battlefield where forty thousand soldiers would die over the next few days. Nine thousand wounded were crammed into the little village—on the streets, the church porches, the stairs of the public gardens—and blood flowed like water on a rainy day. Dunant went several days without sleeping, trying without much success to help these men who had been abandoned by everyone. He never met Napoleon, but on his return to Geneva he wrote in a feverish rush a book that would have a worldwide impact: *Un souvenir de Solferino.* There were numerous editions, and its success was overwhelming, as can be seen from this praise by the Goncourt brothers, who usually did not give themselves over to such things: "These pages filled me with emotion. The sublime reaching to the very fiber of my being. Beautiful, a thousand times more beautiful than Homer, than *La retraite des dix mille,* than anything."[8]

The words are undoubtedly overdone, but they are still symptomatic. Even today one cannot read Dunant's work without emotion. It contains a wonderful idea, a simple idea that, although not new to philosophers, still preserves its great power for the wider public: once they are out of combat because of their wounds, soldiers stop being soldiers. They become again human beings, victims that nothing, not even their nationality, separates. This is the original meaning of the "neutrality" on which the Red Cross was to found its work. In the beginning it was not a question, as in later reproaches, of denying the *political* responsibility of one side or another, but a matter of drawing from this only consideration for the *victims.* Humanitarian law was born, which at first, we sometimes forget, was just one chapter of the rules of war. *Inter arma caritas.* This added two crucial new things in relation to its legitimate ancestors: Christian charity and the philosophy of human rights.

"Do Not Let Happen to Others . . .": The Universal Extension of Charity and Human Rights

A new moral category has appeared between those of good and evil, at the core of newer charitable preoccupations: the *indifference* that has henceforth to be pursued without limit or exclusion, of whatever nature.[9] From now on the 1789 Declaration of the Rights of Man will find itself stripped of the national framework that marked it at its origin—the one through which, in effect, it had to do not only with human beings as such but also with the *citizen,* as a member of a nation with determined historical and geographical contours. From a philosophical point of view, the idea of humanitarian assistance belongs to the universalistic heritage of the declaration. It rests on the idea that all individuals have rights, apart from their being rooted in some particular community—ethnic, national, religious, linguistic, or whatever. But it raises this principle to its highest limit, to the point where the national framework that served as its birthplace tends to vanish. As Jean-Christophe Ruffin puts it:

> To this point, philanthropists such as Florence Nightingale had remained prisoners of their national allegiance. They had agitated for the improvement of the medical services of armies, implicitly considering that it was up to each camp

to take care of "its" wounded. Dunant did not share these nationalistic deformities. He lived, at least in his mind, in an ideal world, and he found it among the wounded heaped up in Solferino. This world of victims was a world of equals; having been struck down by arms, these men had been handed over to it. They had all become neutrals.[10]

Not only will humanitarianism claim to escape national boundaries, in today taking the form of a "right to interfere" it will go so far as to challenge its own highest principle: the sacrosanct sovereignty of states.

As an heir of Christianity and human rights, the humanitarian idea therefore goes beyond them through the exceptional range it gives to the idea of universality. This is what makes it a typical modern and Western notion. It is not that the duty of assistance was unknown to traditional societies. Every moral system, even ancient ones, and certainly every religion has within it the idea of a duty of charity. But most often this remained limited to the particular community defined by each tradition. Solidarity was not voluntarily extended to humanity as a whole, and religious wars did not always bear witness to the greatest compassion. What is more, within Catholicism itself claims to universalism fell under the auspices of proselytism. It was not the other as such who was the object of genuine respect but the potential Christian. Whence the missionary vocabulary of the church, but also the dreadful theses of a "just war" put forth by the greatest Christian theologians. Although it owes much to Christianity, the duty of humanitarian assistance belongs to the space opened, before the French Revolution, by the advent of a secular universe, which, precisely because it breaks with particular traditions, can claim to extend itself to a cosmopolitanism. A new religion was born—that of humanity.

But here, exactly, is where the shoe pinches. If, in principle, the extension of the duty of assistance is infinite (it extends to humanity in general and not just to our close neighbors or our coreligionists) and total (it may require that we sacrifice our lives), how can we reasonably hope to put it in practice? Can the ideal subject of such an obligation be real? It surely calls for a hitherto unknown type of heroic personality, one motivated not by substantial, corporeal values such as love for one's own, one's country, its culture or history, but by respect for pure principles, through a sympathy that can well be called abstract. This surely accounts for the formidable gap between the ideal and the factual. For the "objects" of sacrifice are both much more numerous and farther away than in the past. Every day or so it seems, television news brings new possible targets for eventual activists. And through a similar movement, our motivations for such sacrifice seemingly must dwindle. What solidarity binds me today to a Sudanese, a Cambodian, a Tutsi if not a feeling that is undoubtedly real but essentially abstract of belonging to the same humanity? As Pascal Bruckner has noted, in the face of the images that assail us from every side, we experience the abyss that separates "seeing," "knowing," and "being able to." [11] And this abyss perforce immerses us in a relative indifference. The reason for this, however, may have less to do with the perverse effects of a surplus of information than with the very nature of the humanitarian utopia.

By releasing humans from their old communal bonds, the secularization of the world is the principal source for a universalist ethics. But it implies a double movement that makes its realization difficult, if not improbable. On the one side, we have a divinization of human beings as such. But at the same time, apart from this abstraction, there is no sacred entity, no transcendental value for which sacrifice goes without saying. The new formula of a duty of assistance—"Do not allow to happen to others what you would not want done to you"—perhaps marks some progress in relation to where it comes from. But lacking efficacious intermediaries between the private sphere and the abstract universal, we may well fear that it will remain for the most part a dead letter. Faced with such a fragile enterprise, there is little risk in wagering on the devastating effects of a critique of the entertainment society that, carried out in the style of the sixties revisited, was to reach its apogee during the late eighties.

Humanitarianism in Question

A strange turn of affairs. Just a short while ago, the will to integrate the charitable impulse with politics could pass for a lovely utopian scheme. The creation of a ministry, then the codification by the United Nations of a "right of interference," seemed to crown the efforts of those who, within nongovernment organizations (NGOs), had already long been leading the struggle against the "misfortune of others." Mario Bettati, who along with Bernard Kouchner was one of the founding fathers of this new right, recently pointed to it with a legitimate satisfaction. If the number of NGOs with a charitable purpose has multiplied a hundredfold since 1970, it is because they are responding to a new hope after the foundering of the last political utopias. At the United Nations itself, a resolution of the General Assembly in December 1990 was devoted to the idea of a "fast track" permitting "free access to victims."[12]

Despite what has been accomplished, the billions invested, and the lives saved, the prevailing sentiment today is often negative. All of that has not really done anything; it is merely dust tossed in our eyes, nervous, media-oriented agitation meant to conceal the passivity of northern nations confronted with wars in the East or the South. Saddam Hussein is still there, as is Slobodan Milošević. The genocide in Rwanda happened almost right before our eyes, and everything suggests that the same thing could happen again unhindered in Burundi. The conflict in Bosnia demonstrated Europe's weakness, and the fratricidal battles in Somalia continue after the inglorious departure of the United Nations forces. Exhausted by the interventions of states that sometimes discredit their action, activists who were first on the scene have come to denounce "the predators of humanitarian action" (Xavier Emmanuelli), the "trap" (Jean-Christophe Ruffin), or even the "crime" (Rony Brauman) of an "impossible humanitarianism" (Alain Destexhe). As members of Doctors without Borders, they have spoken out against the confiscation of charitable donations by nations more concerned to restore their tarnished reputations than to act for the good. They have all challenged the emblematic figure of Bernard Kouchner. Has not the founding father and former ally betrayed his own cause by allowing himself to become ensnared in the intrigues of the state and corrupted by the world of images? They agree in their diagnosis. Humanitarianism is not political, nor is it a panacea, and we succumb to a media hoax if we think it can take the place of politics.

That intellectuals and even politicians have taken up this line is easy to understand. Charitable acts as media events have become the most visible symptom of that entertainment society whose foibles it has become a ritual to denounce over the past forty years. They provide an easy target for the right as well as for the left, an almost obligatory one for those who are contemptuous of the world of "media politics." Yet that the sharpest criticism comes from the humanitarians themselves may be what first strikes us as most surprising. Aren't they sawing off the branch they're sitting on? Consider, for example, the opening page of a recent work by Alain Destexhe, secretary-general of Doctors without Borders International:

> Never before has the word [humanitarianism] been such front page news in the press. Never has it been more celebrated, praised, or raised to such heights. Military, political, industrial, artistic, and intellectual leaders rush to its bedside with a flood of good intentions clearly aimed at the media. The craze is widespread. . . . The United Nations has made it one of its principal preoccupations in the post–Cold War period. Closer to us, "reality shows" bring on screen the solidarity of neighbors and the courage of anonymous actors. The public has never been so generous or charitable associations so prosperous. For the moment, this sector has escaped the general sense of crisis in our society. With a permanent escalation of charity, the world no longer knows where to turn its efforts, both of heart and of pocketbook![13]

This is a unique kind of anger, one that stigmatizes the energy it feeds on, a strange turn of events that attacks the generosity of a public it appeals to. In recent times, have we known a more deadly kind of passion? Just a bit more effort, and what it denounces as a craze will have burned out. I wager that such criticism, which itself has become a media event, will have real effects in the coming years, if only in financial terms. Yet however incongruous or misdirected such an attack may seem, it cannot simply be swept aside with the back of the hand. It does, we must admit, have the merit of avoiding demagoguery. It comes not from some intellectual in an ivory tower but from a courageous doctor who has taken part

in operations in the field and who expresses himself with conviction in the name of one of the most recognized organizations. We
must therefore try to understand these criticisms and examine
them more closely to make better sense of just what they mean.
The game is worth the candle in this day when, in the final reckon-
ing, there are not many utopias to be seen.

The Marriage of Ethics and the Media: A Fake Charity?

For self-evident reasons, the principal ally of humanitarian action
is the televised image. In a minimum of time it provides a maxi-
mum of people with the one thing that can mobilize them: indignation and emotion. Above all else, it is through such images that
charitable organizations can hope to bring together the necessary
funds and the energy to carry out their activities. It is also by way
of such images that they can draw attention to themselves and gain
legitimacy. But however indispensable, the tactic is not without its
dangers. For television, we have to say, is not always the best press.
It discredits as much as it legitimates.[14] Enslaved to the constraints
of viewer ratings, to the imperious logic of entertainment, media
culture, and information, if we are to believe what is said, it is well
on its way to hell. For technical as much as for ideological reasons,
speed takes precedence over seriousness, experience over thought,
the visible over the invisible, the shocking image over any idea,
emotion over explanation. In this sense it is the illusions and vanit-
ies of "media society" rather than those of the "cultural state" that
have to be exposed. Sometimes rightly, but often out of a professional bias, a number of intellectuals today are worried by the mea-
ger substantive content presented by television shows, even those
billed as "culture." As for subjects having to do with humanitarianism, they fall into the worst categories. In the end, the only thing
we learn from a televised report is that there is some catastrophe,
some disaster somewhere in the world, victims—who are all equivalent, interchangeable—all equally good for feeding the anxieties
of charitable leaders who themselves have become media stars.
The bottom line, if there is one, is that everything we don't see,
everything that cannot be turned into the object of some image,

will be left out. Which is to say what is essential, beginning with the concrete weight of history and the meanings, in each case particular, that a catastrophic situation contains within itself as soon as we look a bit closer.[15]

The strange thing, once we think about it, is that this calling the media into question often wins approval from intellectuals who themselves are for the most part media personalities. Like the misleading subversions of the sixties to which it is akin, media criticism is a literary genre that easily lends itself to ready-to-wear thinking. If we do not guard against this, it can easily rise to the level of the dominant discourse, readily available to what more or less resembles a marketplace of ideas. This is why it finds its most attentive spokespersons among journalists dealing with cultural affairs.[16] For its impact stems initially from the apparently flattering philosophical perspective it claims to speak from (which comes down to criticizing a mass of morons, alienated by the "entertainment society") while drawing on a thousand little facts taken from real life that confer on it the allure of an unchallengeable empirical truth. In this way it finds an echo in every one of us. There is no intellectual, no journalist conscious of the meaning of the profession, no responsible citizen who has not at some time or another been dismayed by the tomfoolery to be found on the tube. Nor would any one of them not more gladly identify himself with the supposed lucidity of a clearly elitist critical point of view than with that of a populace manipulated by unscrupulous producers. We all can recall recent cases of patent misinformation, nor need one be a leading expert to be able to denounce the stupidity of much that goes on in "prime time." We must even confess that this reality surpasses all the nightmares of any ordinary intellectual critique that sees in it, after the collapse of the habitual targets of cultural leftism, the undreamed-of resurgence of new forms of vexation. Still, it seems to me that we can, even must, renounce the charms of this new rhetoric. Not in order to legitimate things as they stand, from which there is not much to take pleasure, but on the contrary in order to bring our scalpel to the one level where it has some chance of producing a salutary effect.

Let us begin with a diagnosis. When we reproach the news media for wiping out the historical depth of the dramas they present, what are we really talking about? Do we really believe that reports about Bosnia or Somalia have lobotomized a republican, conscientious, and well-informed populace, which has always been brilliant in its incomparable competence regarding the political history of these two countries? What mythical golden age are we referring to here? The reality, by all evidence, is that the vast majority of the public *was not even aware of the existence of* a Bosnia or a Somalia before television took up their fate. The real difficulty is quite other than what is usually suggested when we implicitly measure television news by the yardstick of a course at the Sorbonne. It has to do with the fact that one cannot do the history of Eastern Europe or of Africa every evening. Not only is the audience not the same as the one in the Descartes lecture hall at the Sorbonne, but it has the unfortunate habit of being even more fickle about paying attention. The essential goal of a news report, therefore, can only be first to make people aware of what is going on, then to give them the desire or the courage to take a closer look through the print media or through books. There is an invisible thread that runs from the image to what is written by way of innumerable intermediaries, so it is on its own basis—so to speak from the inside—that we have to judge television, not by comparing it with what it will never be and must never become.

From this point of view, there is no reason to say that televised news reports devoted to these two subjects missed their objective. There were even a few really good programs concerning these conflicts that allowed every viewer if not to form an opinion, at least to realize that we should perhaps at least *try to do something.* Television has played its part. Yes, there has been an emphasis on the spectacular—that is, on the emotional—but also, as much as is possible for images, an incentive to thought and to greater knowledge. Each viewer is given the responsibility, however minimal, of pursuing on his own initiative what is going on. Some may say that such examples are all too rare, and undoubtedly they will be correct. But they do show at least that such things are not impossible. Furthermore, it is not certain that as they multiply to the point of crossing a certain threshold of weariness, something more is not added. We need to be careful about confusing genres. Television will remain a means of entertainment whether we like it or not, but as concerns culture, it has to give rise to thought as well as present things as they are. The image, though, cannot and must not replace the written word.

Objections to what I am saying may then turn to another level, that of ethics. If the virtue of charity counts only because of its disinterested nature, how can it be compatible with the narcissism and the secondary benefits that follow from exposure in the media? In fact, in several ways the question (as regards, say, volunteer work) continues to haunt charitable organizations themselves, to the point that Doctors without Borders, under the influence of Claude Malhuret, ended up by adopting at its general assembly in 1979 a motion stipulating that "the fact of belonging to Doctors without Borders can in no case serve as a means of personal promotion."[17] At that time everyone in the hall knew whom the motion was directed against: Bernard Kouchner, of course, and his project to build on the media hype concerning the "boat people," those unfortunates who at the time were fleeing Vietnam by attempting to cross the South China Sea under truly atrocious conditions. Already at this point, Doctors without Borders was about to split into two factions. On the one side Malhuret, Emmanuelli, Brauman, and Charhon; on the other, Kouchner and his followers, who in many cases had served in Biafra. Beyond personalities (and there were many others, to be sure), beyond the intrigues and quarrels between generations, it was a clash of two "cultures," as Xavier Emmanuelli put it, which did not "measure the media by the same yardstick." For Kouchner, the only way to act was to rouse public opinion. The necessary funds had to be raised quickly to charter a boat, *L'Île de Lumière*, which would become a floating hospital, but also a symbol. Pressure had to be applied to governments so they would welcome the refugees. A prestigious support committee was brought together, including well-known artists and intellectuals. Sartre and Aron found themselves together at the presidential palace defending the project. The significance of that reconciliation, at that moment, was highly symbolic. Those who had supported communist Vietnam rising up to save the boat people, martyrs to that victorious regime! They were even willing to sit at the side of longtime anticommunists, whom they had not so long before called dogs! Solzhenitsyn had been through this mill. Xavier Emmanuelli was hostile to this agitation, which he judged harshly. He published an article titled "A Boat for Saint-Germain-des-Prés" in *Le Quotidien du Médecin,* where, among others, he denounced this "large circle of socialites, aristocrats, mandarins, and other pretentious shapers of opinion" representing tiny Parisian cliques. Put in the minority, Kouchner was to realize this project by other means. And with success—a point we shall see is important. But it was not without sadness that he left the organization he had done so much to bring into existence. From all this was born Doctors of the World.

Fifteen years later, Emmanuelli was still of the same opinion. According to him, the famous boat had served above all else to "make possible a new kind of television, to inaugurate a new heroic spectacle: fiction-reporting live from the scene. The boat for Vietnam did reach its destination. It told a grand and generous tale, opened the way to other such creations, rewarded its promoters. Things turned out well for Saint-Germain-des-Prés." But then comes this incredible admission, which we need to cite word for word and which, in the end, speaks largely in favor of the choice made by Kouchner: "Probably the presence of the boat for Vietnam, loaded with journalists, television reporters, press agencies, and exclusive photographers as well as a few physicians, was able to influence behavior, did save numerous lives, and did incite politicians on all sides to present themselves on screen to make ever more extravagant promises of generosity."[18] Probably "numerous lives"—but wasn't this exactly the sought-for goal, and wasn't the game therefore worth the candle?

From this we can see that as regards this first objection the terms to be weighed cannot, in all seriousness, be put on the same level: on the one side, the venial "sin" of narcissism; on the other the refusal of indifference and the objective necessity, conceded by the critics themselves, to rouse public opinion, which in a democracy is the only thing capable of shaking off government inertia. Is it really necessary, in order to avoid the one, to renounce the others? And who is so pure as to be able to cast the first stone? Our bishops, so prompt today to condemn any excess of zeal, were not fooled. Gathered in plenary session, they too have vigorously denounced "secularization" and the "mediafying" of charity.[19] To each his own role! But let us be frank. By all accounts the problem lies elsewhere, and the objection, however striking it may seem, has little value in the face of the all too real necessities of the "rule of hype." What is more, this does not date back just to yesterday; it precedes the advent of the entertainment society by a long way. Without the media success of Henry Dunant's book, the Red Cross undoubtedly would never have seen the light of day. Indeed, let us not forget what Gustave Moynier had already said at the end of the last century: "The descriptions that daily papers give, so to speak, put the antagonists of the battlefield before the reader's eyes and make his ears ring with both the shouts of victory and the moans and groans of the poor wounded soldiers who fill the ambulances."

Nor is it clear that in denouncing the narcissistic impulses linked to a desire for recognition we really do justice to the feelings and motives that drive them. What are we saying, really, when we declare, as though it were a matter of a condemnation beyond appeal, that it is all a matter of media spin? Let me put things more plainly. We mean that they have given in to a kind of prostitution and believe, with this moralizing evaluation, that we have put an end to the question. Some people even think that in this way they can reach a higher point of view—an ethical superiority, in short—over the individuals they claim to judge. As though in this simplistic manner we could be done with the way the problem of recognition gets posed in an "entertainment society," as though the ancient aspiration to "glory" might not today have motives other than those squalid or cynical ones of ruthless ambition. I think Hannah Arendt came closer to the truth, to another truth at least, in perceiving beneath strategies of winning celebrity an uneasy relation to the mortality of human affairs. For Greek historians, beginning with Herodotus, the task of historiography, in reporting the exceptional deeds of men, was to save them from the forgetfulness that threatens everything that does not belong to the world of nature. Natural effects were cyclical. They repeated themselves just as day follows night and good weather the storm. And their repetition guaranteed that no one could overlook them. The world of nature, in this sense, easily acceded to immortality, whereas "everything that owed its existence to man, such as works, actions, and words were perishable, contaminated, so to speak, by the mortality of their authors." According to Arendt, this was the tacit thesis of ancient historiography when, in reporting "heroic" deeds, it sought to uproot them from the sphere of the perishable in order to make them equal to natural facts.[20] I am not certain that envy and jealousy, so quick to give themselves an air of virtue while prompting the indignant denunciation of other people's behavior, do justice to this residual but patent "metaphysical" dimension of contemporary narcissism.

But perhaps it is not the flaunting of the ego that seems so detestable as much as the "sentimental" vision of the world that charitable ideologies carry along. Based on another objection concealed beneath the first one, this is what comes to annihilate every conceptual effort and any critical perspective.

Emotion against Reflection: An Erroneous Philosophy?

Like television, which it leans on, humanitarianism appeals more to emotions than to reflection, to the heart more than to the head. Following the example of the "Telethon" or "AIDS Week," it tends to be more a spectacle than an analysis, an effective presentation of "good feelings" joined to a suitable dose of guilt presenting images meant to open the hearts and wallets of even the most reluctant viewers. Since it is necessary, let us concede the need for such mobilizing hype. But emotion is not the same as a demonstration, and once the shocking impact of the photos has worn off, what remains in people's heads? What serious comprehension, however small, of the real causes of others' misfortune, be they cultural, historical, or political? Media-based humanitarianism excites public indignation by designating "abstract victims" for its pity, who are all interchangeable. Isn't suffering universal? In the name of the sought-for response, we are to set aside any thought of geographical and historical context.

The background of this second objection must not escape our notice. It is not just a question of denouncing some people's narcissism or even the superficiality of the media; beyond this, there are dangers when emotion governs politics. Many intellectuals have spoken out against this. The primacy of sentiment over intellect has always been a mark of fascist regimes, which demand compliance without any discussion or reflection regarding values or charismatic leaders, not to speak of any *Führer*. Reason and a critical intelligence, that distancing that rightly does not countenance an image, are its natural enemies. Is humanitarianism then a kind of soft fascism?

This criticism seems implacable. However, it misses what is essential. I have already suggested how, from a historical point of view, the idea of humanitarian assistance can be found in the heritage of the Declaration of the Rights of Man. For this declaration really rests on the idea that human beings do possess rights *apart from* their belonging to some particular community, be it ethnic, national, religious, linguistic, or whatever. It is precisely because it adopts this universalistic point of view that humanitarianism has to consider "abstract" victims. But far from this turning into some perverse effect, it is its essence and—let us not mince words—its greatness that are at issue here. By secularizing charity, it reaches beyond traditional forms of solidarity. Happily, it does not choose "its" victims based on communal ties that bind us to them, and this is why context *must* a priori and initially be a matter of indifference.

In *La lenteur*, Milan Kundera's wife, Véra, questions him about Somalia: "Were there also old people dying in that country?" His answer is ironic and disillusioned: "No, no, what was so interesting about that famine, what made it unique among the millions of famines that have happened on earth, is that it cut down only children. We did not see any adult suffering on screen, even if we watched the news reports every day, if only to confirm this never before seen circumstance."[21] What is more, adds this great writer, it was quite logical that it was children who were asked to gather those celebrated sacks of rice so ceremoniously addressed to little Somalians. The sentimental, abstract, media-guided vision of the world is steeped in the infantilism and focus on youth that modern societies are caught up in. Was this a victory for inanity? Dare I say I am not certain it was? How can we not also think, as a kind of counterpoint, of those pages Hans Jonas devotes to childhood in *The Imperative of Responsibility?* He sees in it the archetype that allows us to grasp, in its most original essence, the source of all responsibility toward others. And this for one simple reason, much less "inane" than it might appear to be: a child is not just vulnerable, his vulnerability is a priori, if we can put it this way, a "vulnerability for others." His life cannot continue without the help of adults. It is therefore a sign, as such, without any need for a preliminary detour through reasoning, that points toward *an immediate response on their part.* In this it incarnates, before any explicit request (How can a newborn request anything?), an appeal to others that is not and cannot be marked by any form of reciprocity, as it can be in the world of adults. This is why, according to Jonas, states have toward children who depend on them or who could depend on them "a responsibility distinct from that for the welfare of [their] citizens in general." And he continues, "infanticide is a crime like every murder, but a child's dying of hunger, that is, permitting its starving to death, is a sin against the first and most fundamental of all the responsibilities which man can incur."[22] I would add that in the universalistic perspective that is fortunately that of humanitarian action, the child incarnates par excellence the abstract category of the victim. Not only is his responsibility not a part of the conflicts he dies in, but his belonging to some particular community is also questionable.

In this regard the intervention in Somalia, despite its political and military failure, which everyone rightly acknowledges today, is exemplary. No communal solidarity bound Westerners to the Somalians. No economic or strategic interest was really decisive. It was rather, as Rony Brauman has correctly written, through the pressure of public opinion, via CNN, that the operation was launched. We may regret this but still rejoice in it, for, all things considered, it is one of the beneficial effects of democracies that the people are sometimes more virtuous and stronger than their leaders. And in truth, in the history of humanitarian action from its beginnings I see no other example of intervention that was exempt from some type of traditional, ethnic, or religious solidarity. This is a phenomenon that merits analysis rather than ridicule—which does not, of course, in any way excuse the slowness, the monumental errors, or the mistakes committed by the military.[23] We need to learn the lessons to be drawn from them. But the political and military failure must not lead us to overlook the humanitarian success.[24] Thirty or forty years ago the Somalians would have been allowed to die incomplete silence out of a total indifference—and analogous examples are not lacking. Several hundred thousand people were saved. And from this point of view, on reflection, wasn't the role in public opinion played by emotion stirred up by the media indispensable?

The Alibi of Inaction and Laziness: An Erroneous Politics?

It has been said and repeated to the point of exhaustion: Humanitarianism is not a kind of politics. And of course this is correct. States have their logic, which is not that of good feelings but rather that of power, cynicism, and force. In truth this is not a new discovery. But it generates against a humanitarianism *in* politics, suspected of accrediting the illusion of a "moral politics," a series of objections whose occurrence in the media is so frequent that we need only briefly recall them. By relieving citizens' guilt cheaply (a small check will suffice), humanitarianism turns them away from the necessity of real action, which is first of all social, diplomatic, or military. Furthermore, it runs the risk of dealing with effects rather than causes, of prolonging conflicts and thus the devastation they engender. Once in place, it gives states an alibi for inaction, as we saw in Bosnia, where our Blue Helmets, who were supposed to separate the populations and protect them from the fighting, themselves became hostages. Inefficient state humanitarianism thus threatens private humanitarianism, discrediting it in the minds of those it is meant to help. An erroneous politics, it is also an erroneous kind of justice and law. Not only is interference contrary to the principle of state sovereignty, making some fear a return of a disguised colonialism, but what is more, the interventions it claims to legitimate are arbitrary. Why Somalia or Iraq but not Tibet or Chechnya? Isn't there a double standard at work here? Under the abstraction of "human rights," according to which all victims are equal, clearly there are concealed, unadmitted preferences.

Here once again, things are not as simple as they may seem. For, strictly speaking, we must guard ourselves against lumping under the same opprobrium a deliberate, effectively indecent selectivity and one imposed by necessity.[25] Whether it is a question of government organizations or states, it is clear that it is a more delicate matter to intervene in China or Russia than in Somalia. *Ultra posse nemo obligatur*—no one is expected to do the impossible—was already a maxim of Roman law. But let us be on guard against the illusion that "humanitarian diplomacy" ought to be suppressed, yielding its place to a more traditional kind. There is a great possibility of being deceived. Indeed, nothing allows us to assert that humanitarianism is in competition with, even excludes, military intervention. Does anyone seriously believe that in Bosnia, for example, our European states would have done a better job without any humanitarian action, that it was owing to such activity that they were silent for so long? And can we be certain that fifty years earlier, in the absence of such widespread media hype but also of any real food aid, the city of Sarajevo would not have been wiped off the map in an atmosphere of total indifference? Let us not confuse the cynicism of states that hides behind humanitarianism with its real utility and the nobility it sometimes evinces.

The real difficulty, it seems to me, the one that will have to be resolved in coming years, lies elsewhere. How shall we from here on conceive workable relationships between humanitarian action and politics? Simply to equate them would be absurd and, what is more, would not work in practice. The stands taken by states, whatever they may be, risk jeopardizing the action of private organizations, which is why to this day the Red Cross has maintained the principle of neutrality. Ought we then to separate them completely and, to convey this separation symbolically, abolish the ministry that deals with humanitarian action? This, once again, even if only on a symbolic level, would be to turn politics into cynicism, leaving moral activity to the private sphere alone. This would be a fatal error in a day where, more than ever perhaps, citizens are expressing their willingness to see some ethical aspirations taken into account, that is, *represented,* by the state.[26] No doubt many of us find our political representatives' embarrassment and inability to give any coherent explanation for their lack of action even more shocking than their final decision not to intervene militarily, which made sense in the end (as admitted by the president of Bosnia himself). Thus in the future two things will have to be taken into consideration: if it is true that humanitarianism is not a political program, no longer can a democratic politics do without any reference to humanitarian concerns.

To take this into account we shall have to consider better and more fully than humanitarian spokespeople have done to date those traditional kinds of resistance coming from politics, on the right as well as on the left. For reasons that today have become evident, the political theories of the nineteenth century, in spite of their declarations of principle, were all hostile to international forms of "public charity." For the extreme right, because it held, based on the laws of social Darwinism, that natural selection must be allow to cull the weak; for liberals, because the logic of the market by itself should over time resolve any difficulties; and for Marx, because such a task fell to the revolution. These new forms of theodicy devoted immense effort to evading the central problem that humanitarianism today has again brought before the public: the problem of the persistence of radical evil in a world that calls itself "modern," a world where the great majority of nations have signed the Universal Declaration of Human Rights. Faced with the renewed puzzle of the demonic, our secular societies, lacking adequate words and concepts, have still had to react. In the first place on the grounds of ethics more than on that of politics, but also beyond good and evil on the grounds of *meaning*. Doesn't the struggle against evil, helping to overcome the misfortune of others even at the risk of one's own life in distant countries, at least have the merit of suspending the banality of everyday life? Don't we have here the final word that utopian humanitarianism still exercises despite the criticisms that have been leveled against it? It resounds like a promise of meaning that politics and even moral philosophy tragically cannot offer. And it is not a false promise—at least not wholly false. But it does conceal one trap, the only one, really, whose cunning is subtle enough to challenge philosophical reflection.

Does the Meaning of Life Come through or with Others?

In December 1994, at the initiative of the photographer Roger Job, there appeared a collection of letters meant to lay bare in their plainest, most concrete intimacy the motivations behind the commitment to charitable action. Addressed to families, colleagues, or friends, these brief texts were not written with publication in mind. It was only after the fact, and sometimes many years later, that their authors agreed they could be gathered into a book. It is a book without signatures or any external indications of authorship, hence one arising out of a simple concern to bear witness to a much more complex experience than its contributors could have imagined beforehand. In it we discover with interest and often with emotion the anxieties and joys experienced by those who, out of the most diverse backgrounds and for different reasons, chose to devote a part of their existence to this strange adventure. There is nothing exalted, not to say grandiloquent, about these testimonies, which most often have to do with the details of day-to-day life. Yet again and again, omnipresent between the lines so to speak, is the piercing question of the meaning of each writer's life.

Let us listen to Serge, who in March 1982 writes to his parents from Somalia: "The work is extremely exhausting, but I am madly happy to be a physician, and I finally realize that everything I complained about for seven years does have a purpose. . . . What I am experiencing here is fantastic. I am learning to live again."

Or Alain, working in Chad in February 1986: "I don't understand hate. These soldiers who are killing one another and whom I am taking care of all speak the same language. They have the same customs, often even the same friends. . . . I am sorry I am not able to bring every military trainee here for half an hour. I would show them holes as large as a fist in people's bellies. I would make them listen to the cries of pain. I would make them smell the stink of pus and shit that goes with combat in the name of a badly understood ideal."

Whether evaluated positively or negatively, humanitarian action is perceived by those who practice it as loaded with experience, lessons, and meaning. Thus as Rony Brauman says in the preface he wrote for this collection, in it one experiences "the happiness, in the first place, of having snatched a life from the grasp of death, of having added a bit of meaning to one's own life." And the former president of Doctors without Borders emphasizes: "Beyond the great debates over the new—or papered over—world order, over the cynicism of the powerful or the universality of morality, beyond their fears or their frustrations, [the humanitarians] know that their choice places them among the last really privileged people of modernity—those who have been able to give a meaning to their lives."[27]

Is this a meaning gained *through others?* No doubt it is, since it is part of the very structure of meaning that it is given to us in our relationship to the other. But for all that, ought we to accept, without any further qualification, the equation whereby saving a life comes down to justifying one's own?[28] Maybe. I do not claim to be able to judge. Simply, it seems to me that this hypothesis contains within it still more questions. To my mind, if there is a "humanitarian trap," it is the one that lies in an erroneous interpretation of "meaning through others." This is a risk that Hegel had already listed under the category of the "bad infinite": the need constantly to seek meaning—out of some lack, so to speak—in an ever-receding alterity. The misfortune of others ought never to serve as a pretext, however noble it may seem, to hide our own misfortunes, and sometimes it is more courageous to work at home and on our own than to traipse around the world. There is a Don Juanism of charity in seeking to find our own meaning through others. This would be a hopeless undertaking if the task, which gets confused with all the unhappiness in the world, is just as inexhaustible, so that meaning remains forever ungraspable.

Generosity presupposes riches. It overflows and radiates to others rather than nourishing only itself. At least this is what Aristotle teaches in his *Nicomachean Ethics.* To be generous, he asserts, one must be wealthy. Often (mis)understood as the sign of a contemptuous aristocracy, this proposition evokes the parable of the talents: "Nor will the one who wishes to make use of it to help others neglect his patrimony."[29] To cultivate our patrimony: it is also within ourselves and not just in others that we have to learn to recognize transcendence and the sacred. It is in ourselves and not just through others that we have to learn to preserve them against the crossfire of dogmatic religions and materialist anthropologies. This is the necessary condition if we are to live not just *through* or *for* others, but also *with* them.

If humanitarianism carries a meaning, it seems to me, it cannot content itself with its negative aspect, that of only an "ethics of urgency" (of self-justification by way of others' misfortune). It cannot fail to reflect on the possibilities of rediscovering outside traditional religions a *meaning in common* with those whose suffering and dignity rightly appear to it as sacred. It has to renew its ties, even beyond the ethics that animates it, with those places that traditionally were the site of a life in common, of culture and politics. And if it teaches us to recognize the sacred in human beings, it must also incite us to seek out the way this new face of meaning can and must irradiate a democratic culture and politics for which disenchantment today *seems to be* the principal characteristic. Wrongly, perhaps.

The Reassumption of the Sacred into Culture and Politics

No doubt it is within the sphere of art that the ending of a religious grounding of norms and values has produced the most obvious reversals. It is also here that the reassumption of the sacred may best be able to permit the renewal, so long expected since the clinical death of avant-garde movements, of a world common to people of today. In fact, too often we continue to live in cultures belonging to the past, far distant from contemporary forms of art, which themselves remain still too distant from their public. We really ought to speak of an end of the "theological-cultural" in order to rightly name the extraordinary mutation that has characterized modernity, at least since the seventeenth century. It is impossible to comprehend our present situation with regard to works of art unless we can grasp the key moments of this evolution in terms of its guiding principle. To keep things simple, we can describe them as follows.

In past civilizations works of art had a sacred function. Even within ancient Greece their mission was to reflect a cosmic order external to human beings and superior to them. It was owing to their exteriority that they took on a quasi-religious dimension, if it is true that the divine is essentially what escapes human control and transcends it. These works were in the etymological sense a "microcosm," a little world held to represent on a reduced scale the harmonious properties of the whole universe that the ancient Greeks named the cosmos. It was from this that these works drew their "imposing" grandeur. They were "imposing" in the literal sense owing to their capacity to *impose themselves* on individuals, who received them as coming from outside themselves. A work of art thus possessed "objectivity." It expressed not so much the genius of the architect or sculptor as the divine reality it conveyed to human beings. Even today, we are so much aware of this that it does not really matter to us whether we know the name of the artist who made the bronze cats in our halls of Egyptology. What counts is that the cat is a sacred animal, transfigured as such into the space of art.

It is not saying much to admit that our situation with regard to art has changed. It has even inverted itself to the point where the name of an artist may be more familiar to us than his works. To be convinced of this we need only think about the attitude toward contemporary music of that public we call "cultivated." The names of composers sometimes attain a notoriety that is denied to their compositions. Compare this to the fact that the German middle class in Leipzig could listen to the music of Bach without the slightest concern for who wrote it. Nietzsche's assertion that the truth of art is to be found in the artist has been realized beyond all expectations. A work of art is no longer the reflection of a harmonious, extrahuman world, but rather the expression of the personality of a singular, exceptional individual—a genius who draws from his inner riches the stuff of his creations.

The crisis today affecting every avant-garde cannot be understood apart from this subjectivizing of art. No doubt this has to do with the belated effects of the internal contradiction directly implied by the idea of an absolute innovation. For as Octavio Paz perceived early on, the gesture of breaking with tradition, the ideal of the tabula rasa, has itself become a tradition at the end of this century. The subversive signs that mark the history of the avant-garde no longer surprise us. They have become banal, democratic to the point of being taken into museums to be placed side by side with the most classical forms of art. What is more, just like the republican schoolteacher of yesteryear, the avant-garde artist thought it his task to carry out a great revolution in order to extirpate from our hearts and minds any taste for the last vestiges of tradition. As a French specialty, avant-gardism shares with anticlericalism, to whose form it is so akin, this concern to wipe out the remnants of the past in order to emphasize the new as new. It was owing to this movement that it was led to exalt subjectivity, to cultivate original- ity for the sake of originality.

For better or worse, our secular universe tends therefore to re- fuse any reference to what is external to human beings in the name of an ever increasing demand for autonomy. Isn't it normal under these conditions, then, that art itself has given in to the imperative of being on a "human scale," in every way a human creation meant for human beings?

Everything would be fine in the best of all possible worlds if this humanistic aspiration had not ineluctably turned into the ever more pressing question, Is there, can there be, a "modern gran- deur" in the double sense of being a measure of greatness? Isn't this self-contradictory? For isn't grandeur indissolubly linked to the representation of a transcendent universe, external to individuals, and for that reason *imposing?* How can what is only immanent to humanity still possess this sacred character in the absence of which everything is just entertainment and vanity—or at the very least, familiar proximity? While yet a theology student, Hegel asked himself what the "religion of a free people" would be. In asking this he meant to reflect on the conditions under which humanity could finally *recognize itself* in some common culture, freed of all dogmatism and that opaque exteriority that sums up "arguments from authority." He thought that Christianity had to free itself from its "positivity," from everything in it that remained refractory to the human spirit. But from the point of view of tradition this meant suppressing religion itself, forcing it into the mold of mere reason. And if art too is sacred, "a sensory presentation of the di- vine" or of its symbols, how can we avoid admitting, as Hegel did, that along with religion it fell into the bleak category of outdated cultural forms?

Thus we live at the end of the age of the exalted, at least in the sense we have been discussing. What philosopher of my generation would dare to compare himself to Plato and Aristotle—or, closer to us, even to Spinoza, Kant, or Hegel—without smiling, not to say laughing? What composer would claim to be today's Mozart or Beethoven? What politician, without going any further back in history, would compare himself to Clemenceau, de Gaulle, or Churchill? And why are these simple examples, which could easily be multiplied and adapted to everyone's taste, so telling to anyone with any sense at all? Is it due to a lack of historical distance? The intellectual downfall of humanity? I don't think so. Moreover, we need only turn to scientists to see that the situation there looks very different to us. We would have no difficulty there in listing many great minds. As seems obvious, it is classical culture, that of the humanities, that has changed its status, since the very moment it began to cut itself free from religion.

We must, I insist, keep coming back to this question: If the source of every work of art is human, hence from a traditional point of view (and without turning it into too facile a formula) all too human, isn't secular culture also destined to situate itself at the same level? And isn't this also the origin of all the arguments today that begin from a pessimistic diagnosis of the decline, defeat, or decadence of contemporary culture? With the eclipse of the vertical dimension of the sacred, isn't it, in the literal sense of the term and without meaning it as a value judgment, dullness that threatens us? How are human beings to draw from within themselves, without any reference to a radical beyond more imposing than themselves, the stuff of any modern grandeur? This, I believe, is the crucial question at the end of our century. Haven't the most important people—whether politicians, philosophers, or artists—been those who above all else incarnated sublime things: divinity, patriotism, reason, revolution? But if I no longer represent anyone other than myself—if I am, in Sartre's words, someone who is the equal of all others and to whom all others are equal—how can I claim to institute that "grand style" or that "great politics" Nietzsche called for? If we refuse, as this book asks us to do, to give in to any nostalgia for times immemorial where the transcendence of the divine, however illusory it may have appeared to be, could imprint the trace of the sacred on the most humble of human works, toward what sublime horizon should we lift our eyes?

Considering those areas of life that escape the contingencies of taste and sensibility may, I believe, point us on our way. Sports, for example, a democratic spectacle if ever there was one, but fascinating for their capacity to reconstitute aristocratic glories in a world that essentially has been stripped of them. This example may seem out of bounds, not to say trivial, when it comes to finding some analogy for high culture. But consider this: competition in sports rests above all on the principles of egalitarianism so dear to modern humanism. The rules are the same for everybody, as is the equipment used, to the point that cheating, which introduces inequalities, symbolizes the crime that is unacceptable to everyone. Yet hierarchies do reconstitute themselves there from a purely human base and even, it must be said, a certain grandeur. Some players really surpass others, unexpectedly and in inexplicable ways, and they arouse admiration. Yes, this is a partial transcendence, but it gives an image—and it is only a question of such an image— of an unfathomable human grandeur. Why shouldn't we be able to find the same thing in the realms of culture and politics?

The Two Faces of Politics as a "Technique": The Cult of Performance and That of Technology

Why does a "democratic melancholy" so easily take hold of people who apparently are well off? Are our peaceful democracies so uninspiring that we ought to feel no attachment to them? Countermodels certainly are not lacking. From Algeria to Iran, from Serbia to Rwanda, from Sudan to India or Cambodia, passing through Egypt, fundamentalisms of all kinds have bloodied countries with such ferocity that we may well congratulate ourselves for living in a privileged situation. Certainly there are unemployment, new forms of poverty, and no doubt other serious deficits to acknowledge. Nothing can excuse them or make us overlook them. But they apply to the rest of the world too, and let me dare to suggest that it may be better to be unemployed in Bonn or Paris than to be a worker in Bombay or Saint Petersburg. Given the current state of things, the will to extend to the whole world the humanist and secular system that has proved itself in postwar Europe looks for many reasons like an ambitious project, not to say a utopian ideal. Fidelity to human rights, political liberty, peace, a relative prosperity, respect for other cultures, and self-criticism—isn't this an ideal our modest continent might offer to the rest of the world as something it might well be inspired by?

No doubt others' misfortune is not the best way to convince ourselves of our own good fortune. A few malcontents even think that, far from relativizing it, such misery should add to our sense of well-being. However that may be, there is one basic reason any comparison with different societies cannot suffice to justify our way of life. Today it is from *within* its own borders that the West has begun to perceive the flaws that its opposition to hostile regimes, in particular communism, has for a long time permitted it to overlook.[30]

Whence, in parallel with the death of avant-gardes, the nagging complaint about the "end of great plans" and the need to rediscover the urgency that goes with them. A politician in an Islamic republic can claim to draw his strength from the fact that he incarnates a figure of the absolute. The head of a nationalist state still holds the possibility of representing in the eyes of his people the incomparable genius of his nation, a sacred entity because it is superior to its members. When de Gaulle died, the press did not hesitate to print a headline that said "France a Widow." I very much doubt that such a slogan would apply to any of today's politicians, and even less, I think, to tomorrow's, so strong has been the desacralizing of the idea of the nation. The revolutionary leader preserved, for better or worse, the sense of incarnating a sacred mission. God, country, revolution—all consecrated great plans. How can the secular, democratic politician, by comparison, not fail to look like some small-time office manager? In the best of cases we acknowledge in him the virtues of competence and integrity, but how can these justify the exorbitant pretension that he inherits, willingly or not, of raising himself above the ordinary run of morals in order to serve as their guide? He feels the urgency to formulate some vast project; his followers all urge him on. But where are we to find that "great political leader" in a universe where the wellspring and the horizon are so humanized that nothing in it can rise to the level of the sacred without contravening its secular and democratic ideals?

By default, therefore, politicians choose to try to stay in power. And since we live in a democracy, they will do so using every

means allowed by this kind of regime. Without having seen it coming, in the past few years we have entered the age of politics as a
technique, in the philosophical sense, a search for ways to increase
the *means* of power to the detriment of any reflection on its *ends*, an
art of mastery for the sake of mastery, of domination for the sake
of domination. It is not by chance that the name of one such suc-
cessful person, François Mitterrand, symbolizes the two most far-
reaching effects of the period we have just come through: on the
one hand, the liquidation of the traditional ideas of the left, which
each person can evaluate as he wants;[31] on the other, the laying
bare of the mechanisms of a politics run by expert technicians,
whose expertise allowed our president to remain in office longer
than anyone else in the history of our republic. On the one hand,
the death of "objective reason," of that reason that determines
ends, actually "objectives," and that does not limit itself just to tac-
tical or strategic considerations; on the other, the consecration of
"instrumental reason" and Machiavellianism.

Technology—that is the key word. But we need to grasp its exact sense. Heidegger traced its true origin back to the emergence
of modern, Cartesian science, which promised human beings the
domination of the universe. Progress of civilization through the
progress of reason—this was the spirit that drove the whole philosophy of the Enlightenment. But with this belief we are still far from
the "world of technology" properly speaking, from that universe
where any consideration of ends vanishes to the exclusive profit of
a consideration of means. In the rationalism of the seventeenth
and eighteenth centuries, the project of a scientific mastery of nature, then of society, still had an emancipatory intent. In principle,
it remained subject to the realization of certain *goals*. If there was
a question of dominating the universe, of making us its "masters
and owners," this was not out of fascination with our own strength
but in order to attain certain objectives that bore the names of
liberty and happiness. And in relation to these ends, the development of the sciences appeared to our ancestors as the bearer of
another form of progress as well: morals. Illusory this might have
been, but it was not Machiavellian.

For our worldview to become thoroughly technological, therefore, another step was required. The will had to stop considering

ends external to itself and to take itself, so to speak, as its own object. According to Heidegger this is what happened in philosophy, with Nietzsche and his concept of the will to power as the metaphysical foundation of the planetary technology we swim in today. Indeed, for Nietzsche the authentic will, the accomplished will, is the one that stops willing *something* in order to become a "willing of willing," a will that seeks the increase of vital forces—that is, of its own growth, of its own intensification as such. In this way the will reaches the perfection of its concept. Willing itself, it becomes mastery for the sake of mastery, force for the sake of force, and stops being subject to external ends, as it still was in the progressive ideal of the Enlightenment.

It is difficult, I believe, not to accept the diagnosis according to which our political life finds itself caught up in this technological way of seeing things. It is significant that, on the reelection of François Mitterrand in 1988, the newspaper *Libération* ran the headline "Bravo l'artiste!" saluting in this way the performance *for its own sake* even though the actor in question would, in a single seven-year term, wipe out the quasi totality of those ideas this left libertarian newspaper had been based on since its founding. Against such a crazy consecration of technology in politics, we need to regain our senses, to somehow make it possible for our fellow citizens to again look themselves in the eye without shame or fear, so that hate will no longer be the most appropriate term to describe the atmosphere of our slums. I am convinced that a good number among them are ready to accept the rigor that has to come—to make, as so often said, sacrifices. But for this to happen they must have the sense of committing themselves to a cause that is somehow transcendent and sacred, the sense that the sacrifices agreed to are not meant to serve instrumental reason, allowing those in power to remain in power, but rather are part of a collective project to restore decent, not senseless, relations among people.

In this respect the shift from a vocabulary of performance to the still technocratic one of *constraint* has not been a success. It is not enough to oppose the courage of realism to the demagoguery of instrumental reason if people—that is, all of us—are to make sense of a more committed politics. Just think for a moment about the way these much talked about constraints are usually presented, in the language of "reasonable" politicians as well as most opinion makers. We must, we are told, reduce our deficits, be "virtuous," in order to meet the criteria for the construction of Europe (the Maastricht Treaty, a single currency, etc.). Well and good. But has anyone thought for even a second about the fact that no citizens outside a very narrow elite can grasp why these are necessities, any more than they can grasp the final purpose of a single currency? That none of them have read the treaty in question or can recognize themselves in *any of the European institutions whose alpha and omega they are unaware of?* Or we hear this: We have to take account of the "financial markets that affect us," because "interest rates" will not go down unless we do the right things. I have no intention, it goes without saying, of contesting to however small an extent the validity of these assertions; I only say loud and clear that, despite having more than one academic degree and a real interest in political questions, I am like 99 percent of my fellow citizens: absolutely ignorant about the mechanisms that govern the world of international high finance. Like everyone else, therefore, I tend to fall back on somewhat mechanical images or representations of what I hear about almost every day. But what is the meaning of all this?

To what supposed base of knowledge does a politics that opposes technological realism to technical demagoguery appeal (no doubt rightly, but that is not the question)? Economics is not a required subject in our schools, and this "science" seems so shaky even to those who claim to understand it that no consensus seems likely to emerge. I would like to suggest that our political leaders take a poll to see what French people, even those with a good education, know about the Council of Europe or the CAC 40,[32] that strange being that invites itself to dinner with our fellow citizens every evening through the medium of television news. Perhaps they would learn how unreasonable it is to hope to make their plans meaningful by founding what interests everybody on what interests nobody, and for good reason! All the more so, and making things more difficult, with the structure of Europe today we have lost the framework in which the connection between democracy and solidarity was forged—the national framework. Here again I do not mean to deny the necessity for a Europe that is supposed to allow the older nations to still play a role. But isn't it crazy to underestimate the price of such "progress"? It was within the nation-state, and so far as I can see nowhere else, that *particular* individuals were able to recognize themselves, through their political standing, in the representation of something that in some small way resembled the *general* interest. And it is in terms of this framework that some kinds of solidarity still hold. Therefore we cannot, without flagrant contradiction, deplore the disappearance of the res publica and the rise of corporate entities while at the same time favoring the eradication of the one known space where the former could find its place and the other be held in check. Not without wanting to have our cake and eat it too, all the while keeping the baker smiling. In the current state of affairs, the construction of Europe remains a "subjectless process." It does produce laws, commercial exchanges, and bonds of all sorts among peoples, *but without this production's being visible at any moment, or a fortiori comprehensible by its citizens. Irresponsible,* in the literal sense, it cannot be imputed to any subject—not to one person, since there is no president, not to some national sovereignty, since there is no parliament worthy of the name. Yet we want Europe to be today's great project, one that will give meaning to politics following the collapse of ideologies? Is this really, given the way things are, reasonable?

Between the demagoguery of technicians and a technocracy, however intelligent and well-intentioned, between the cult of performance and capitulation to "objective constraints," modern politics must invent new ways. It must renew its ties with the meaning it lost with the secularization of the world. Constraints are what they are—it's their nature. Yet is it any less inconceivable that, for a country as rich as ours, utopia consists solely in reducing the number of unemployed by two hundred thousand people a year, as one recent candidate for the presidency of the republic asserted? Isn't this in the end, and at the end of a seven-year term, to set an objective that would still in the best of cases leave two to two and a half million individuals outside that common space of meaning that is supposed to constitute any national community? A realistic politics cannot content itself with such a sorry undertaking. Otherwise it will immediately hand things over to the demagoguery of the technicians. We need to explore new ways, perhaps those of sharing work, of distinguishing between productive and useful activities; we need to invent different forms of solidarity than that RMI that avoids the worst case but does not bring any dignity or occupation to its beneficiaries.[33] I can already hear the chorus of disenchanted liberals. Be careful: to rediscover transcendence, wouldn't that be to reinstitute one of those utopias that are all the more dangerous and deadly for being so seductive and motivating? Isn't it to reintroduce, in whatever form you like, the old dogmatic principle of arguments from authority? And isn't the meaning that gets so readily associated with the idea of transcendence a distant cousin of the "meaning of history," in whose name so many crimes have been committed?

The Reenchantment of Politics: Implanting *Dikē* in *Philia*

To rediscover meaning: perhaps this formula sounds like a dangerous or empty slogan. How many times have we heard our politicians, and with them a few intellectuals, refer to the necessity, or should I say, the urgency of "finding a new big project," of "reinventing politics," of "restoring real distinctions," of "reopening the future," and so on and on. And how many times have we wanted simply to retort, "Well, go ahead, do it. Stop being so worked up, for goodness sake!" What then follows, of course, are endless hollow incantations about building a "more solidary, more just, more humane society" that will fight against "exclusion," ensure the promotion of human rights and the protection of nature in a "global, planetary" context of solidarity among peoples, and so on. Let's be honest. Is there is a politician, much less an intellectual, who can begin this kind of speech today without strongly encouraging the natural tendency of our fellow citizens to click their remotes? Such words, however noble, are worn out. The politics of experts with its double face—of the cult of performance, carried to absurdity in the press with its talk of rises and falls in the polls, and the technocratic one of constraints that are imperceptible to the ignorant many—has led not only to masking the social dimension,[34] or even to liquidating the left's most classical themes, but finally to discrediting the very idea of ideas in politics.

All the more so in that the justice in question, ever since the end of theological ethics and the retreat of every form of communitari-anism, has lost its concretely perceivable, corporeal dimension to become a matter of *laws*. Here lies the grandeur of secular moral-ity, but also its Achilles' heel.[35] Under the control of the state, elab-orated by national representatives, the law must inevitably remain abstract. The difficulty does not have to do, as is often unreflec-tively claimed, with the definitions given it here or there, differ-ently on the right and on the left, and marked by those much dis-cussed "distinctions" that allow us to escape forcing everyone to think alike. In truth, the well-known theory proposed by John Rawls applies nicely to the great majority of cases.[36] A just society is one that, first, respects formal liberties, and second, turns out to be more favorable than any other to the least favored of its mem-bers. One final point, or as much of it as is required. The real challenge is not theoretical but both practical and spiritual. If we want to give, not "regive," meaning to a disenchanted politics, we have first of all to ask ourselves about those concrete places where meaning comes from for individuals who no longer believe in the virtues of the state. The answer, I think, is hard to doubt. It is *philia* today that most determines the meaningfulness of our lives. So long as politics continues to underestimate the historical impor-tance of the birth of modern life, it will not understand the extraor-dinary potential of solidarity, of the *sympathy* that dwells within the private sphere. And as long as it does not base itself on this, it will elicit no enthusiasm.

Some will object—some already have—that a "turn to the pri-vate sphere" cannot lie at the origin of a new political vision, since this would represent its most radical negation. And others will emphasize, in this context, how much the reigning individualism is by nature hostile to the reconstitution of collective "great plans." But that, I believe, is the great error. For, in truth, there is no oppo-sition between *philia* and *dikē* (justice), between the sacralization of love and *private* friendships, on the one hand, and, on the other, a concern for a *universal* justice. On the contrary, it is by basing our-selves on feelings that we can give the law that substantial dimen-sion that it has lost because of its separation from earlier forms of community.

Someone will even object to this. One cannot be too mistrustful about feelings in politics; the virtue of the law lies exactly in its transcendence of changing or impulsive moods. In seeking to reinstall it in human hearts, we risk a confusion of genres that will take us back to ancient conceptions of justice, not to say to totalitarianism. Yes, we do need to be careful, and if the law is to provide a stable framework it must not reduce to moods. We must not let the Jewish element get swallowed up in the Christian one, let law be dissolved into love.[37] But who is talking about a "dissolution" here? A reconciliation will suffice. All the more so in that the feelings whose historical emergence I am referring to here are not merely *psychological* or, as Kant would have put it, *pathological*. They testify, as I have tried to show, to a new relation to the sacred—a transcendence inscribed in the immanence of human subjectivity, in the space of a humanism of man made god.

The Humanism of Humanity Made God

Is Christianity a humanism? Undoubtedly, since it places human beings at the center of creation and grants them the most eminent place within this worldly order—that of a being created in the image of God. Yet the pope's question about the reestablishment of a moral theology anchored in the "splendor of truth," which would stand over against civil law if need be, has to trouble Christians attached to the principles of democratic humanism. For example, how can we reconcile the assertion that abortion is murder with accepting a positive law that authorizes its practice? Who is to be obeyed? We can try to distinguish between rights and morality, between the public sphere of law and the private one of conscience. But the distinction does not hold in the case of murder and turns out to be insufficient for anyone who wants to be faithful to the teachings of the magisterium. It is just this distinction that John Paul II wants us to challenge. And *from this point of view*, theological humanism, that very humanism that defends the absolute value of human life, ceases being a juridical and political one. Against the grounding of laws in the will of a people gathered in secular assembly, it reasserts the primacy of divine commandments.[1] Instead of anthropocentrism, it enjoins us to return to theocentrism. Therefore the question whether we can say that Christianity is a humanism remains largely open, depending on how we formulate it.

The same can be said, in my opinion, about atheistic humanism, which for the sake of argument I have associated with the way lawyers talk. I hope they will forgive me, or at least grant that there are extenuating circumstances. To be sure, it is a metaphorical usage. But in some respects the determinism to which they are so often forced to appeal, it seems, could well claim the name of humanism. It also leads toward atheism and materialism. And isn't it this latter that finally allows us to cross the threshold that leads away from that theocracy by means of which human beings are constantly turned back in the direction of a heteronomy of norms? This is what Nietzsche, with his habitual perspicacity, announced to us along with the death of God. I have already shown how, as a genuine materialist, he situated the essence of all religion in the recognition of values "higher than life." This assertion perfectly defines the outlines of what could become a radical humanism, an anthropocentrism stripped of the illusions of theology. Furthermore, it was in a book with the provocative title *The Twilight of the Idols* that he most clearly articulated this position: "Judgments, judgments of value, concerning life, for it or against it, can, in the end, never be true: they have value only as symptoms, they are worthy of consideration only as symptoms; in themselves such judgments are stupidities."[2] For, he adds, the value of life *cannot be estimated* either by anyone alive, because he is both judge and interested party, or clearly, by anyone dead.

As is so often the case with Nietzsche, the argument is a bit laconic. So it will be helpful to lay out its points. They will then be able to serve as a philosophical foundation from which to judge every form of reductionism. Nietzsche's argument represents in this regard the greatest assault ever conducted by thought against the idea of transcendence. What does Nietzsche mean, and why has it had so many echoes? First of all this: In order to judge life it is necessary to adopt a situation *external* to it, to be able to posit, outside life, the frame of reference in terms of which we can make any judgment. It is necessary to presuppose an ideal transcendent sphere, a beyond, a distance starting from which there will be some meaning to making evaluations. But this is the supreme illusion, the illusion par excellence of all religion. Humans are living beings among other such beings; they clearly *belong* to life, they are immanent to it, which is why their supposed judgments are only symptoms, unconscious manifestations of a *certain type of existence.* There is no "metalanguage," no higher discourse in the name of which it would be possible to determine the meaning and value of the world we find ourselves caught up in.

From this we can see how Nietzsche traces out the way that will be at least the dominant one of the human sciences. It is their task to demonstrate, using facts and arguments, how the fantasy of transcendence arises. With Durkheim, sociology will uncover the last stronghold of this positing of a beyond. It is because the whole is more important than the parts, because society is stronger than any individual, because it transmits its values to them that they so readily yield to the illusions of the sacred. But this sacred is never anything other than a disguised form of the collective conscience. For Freud the origin of this mythology is to be found within the individual unconscious, with, in the end, an analogous if not identical outcome: religion is just the obsessional neurosis of humanity. Sociobiology and the genetic study of behavior will then complete the picture by referring to "brotherhood genes" and explaining the genesis of altruism by the history of natural selection. In a general way the human sciences, the resistance of a few mavericks aside, will lead to reductionism. Their argument will repeat Nietzsche's. The illusions of transcendence are born when we project outside ourselves what in reality is only an unconscious part of ourselves. They stem from that fetishism that Marx showed consisted in granting objectivity to what is always only a product of social, psychological, or natural history. It is because these histories "surpass" us that they can sometimes convey a sense of the sacred. Against any such intellectual laxness, human beings must constantly be called back to immanence, verticality must constantly be brought down to horizontality. And if people do not willingly consent to such things, it is of course because of "resistances" linked to their unconscious. These resistances have to be overcome, and then humanity will accede to itself. Unalienated, human beings will become what they really are.

This, more or less, is the type of argument in whose name atheistic materialism can claim to advance under the banner of humanism against a Christianity that appears unduly to claim that banner as its own. For at least two reasons it seems to me that this title does not belong to atheistic materialism any more than to Christianity.

First, as I have already suggested, because in annulling a priori and in principle any possible reference to a transcendence of any kind whatever, the argument dissolves human beings into their context. Nietzsche, by the way, was not deceived by this and surely would have refused the proposed banner. It still comes down to the myth of an autonomous, free individual. But human existence is only one fragment among others of the will to power. The human sciences confirm this by adding to the Nietzschean reduction to life that of the god History. Humans are not the authors of their acts or their ideas; they are in every respect only a *product*.

Next, because materialism is always marked by what contemporary logicians call a "performative" contradiction, it forgets its own position in stating its theses. Like someone who claims to be the victim of a catastrophe that no one survived, it denies its subjectivity at the very moment it claims to state the truth. The sophism stands out clearly in Nietzsche's assertion that every judgment about life is a symptom. Are we to understand this to be a "true" proposition (which would contradict his thesis) or in its turn as a mere symptom (which would then deny it any claim to the truth)? Because of this contradiction, which always affects the dominant discourse of the human sciences, reductionism constantly puts anyone who defends it in disagreement with himself. In the content of his discourse he is a relativist, who denounces transcendence and affirms the weight of history and of those unconscious determinations of different contexts to which he claims to give us access. But in his heart of hearts he is, like everyone else, convinced of the truth of his discoveries and his assertions, in which he sees not illusory or misleading symptoms but rigorous logic, completely independent of his own unconscious. He makes an exception for himself, in short, reintroducing his free subjectivity without being able to take it up for what it is. And it is this negation of the real person that takes from materialism the possibility of claiming clearly to be a humanism. Which is why its rallying to the theme of the "death of man," supposed to follow immediately from that of the death of God, is so pertinent.

The humanism whose face I have attempted to draw stands in a completely different tradition of thought. Its relation to the Christian religion is more nuanced, since it rejects neither the sacred nor transcendence, even if it does refuse to conceive of them in the dogmatic mode of a theological ethics. I must now attempt, if not to complete the picture, at least to give it color.

"Transcendental" Humanism

Let us begin with its tradition, which to be sure is that of Rousseau and Kant, but also of Cartesianism as revisited by Husserl and Levinas. These names by themselves do not say anything—or rather, they say too much. We need to be more precise. Here is what in my opinion they have in common and what situates them at the origin of what I am here calling "transcendental" humanism: the positing of what is proper to humankind "outside nature." "Outside nature"—that is, also outside the determinism that governs natural phenomena. This means affirming the mystery at the heart of humanity, its capacity to free itself from the mechanism that rules overall in the nonhuman world and that allows science to know it thoroughly and to make predictions about it. For Rousseau and Kant this is to be found in the definition they give of human freedom: an unfathomable faculty to oppose oneself to the logic, so implacable for other animals, of "natural inclinations." It can be found again in Husserl in his critique of that "psychologism" and "sociologism" in whose name the human sciences would like to reduce our behavior to a physics of ideas and emotions. It is also, finally, what Heidegger, Levinas, and Arendt all affirm in their different ways when they define the *humanitas* of humankind in terms of "transcendence" or "ek-sistence"—a capacity to raise oneself above "ontic" or "intraworldly" determinations so as to penetrate the sacred domain of the "thoughtful life."

Is it irrational to posit the mystery of freedom, to thereby oppose oneself to the logic of reductionism, which asserts and ceaselessly reasserts the law of causality and "the principle of reason"? We know today—or we ought to know—that the argument is, as mathematicians put it, "undecidable." The principle in question is in essence irrefutable, "unfalsifiable" in Popper's sense of this term. Indeed, it is impossible to refute the deterministic hypothesis that our actions, attributed to the effect of a mysterious freedom and in this very way posited as something more in relation to nature, could be secretly brought about by some unconscious motivation. This, to be sure, is the very essence of that seductive force that emanates from the deterministic human sciences. They appeal to something invisible and claim, against the naïveté of illusions about consciousness, finally to be able to make them visible. Demystification is always enjoyable. But this is also their weakness. Because it itself is not refutable, their fundamental postulate, that of a hidden rationality, is not itself scientific. It stems from a metaphysical bias and is, as such, one belief among other beliefs. Whence the possibility of a "practical faith" in the existence of freedom. If good and bad have a meaning, if at least they ought to have one, I have to be able to presuppose that human beings are capable of choosing between them. To be convinced of this we need only reflect a contrario. Let us imagine a being who would be, like an destructive robot, infallibly programmed to kill, without having within itself the slightest possibility of making another choice. Such a being would certainly be a problem, but it would not properly speaking be evil. We could undertake to destroy it, but we could not blame it for its actions, which it could not, given our hypothesis, avoid committing. Since it is not endowed with the quality that transforms a being into a *person*, its acts would have no meaning, as symbolized by the metallic voice and glassy eyes rigged up in science fiction films.

The argument is an old one. All the arguments are already known, and every attempt to renew them makes me think of those famous chess games people replay in imitation of the grand masters. The moves are predictable. I don't want to dwell on this point, which I have dealt with elsewhere.[3] I want merely to underscore in what sense today the bias in favor of freedom—for it is a matter of a bias, of a postulate—implies a humanistic reinterpretation of the principal concepts of the Christian religion. The cardinal opposition is not, as has long been thought, between a dogmatic religion on the one side and deterministic materialism on the other, between clericalism and anticlericalism. The refusal of arguments from authority is an acquired fact, something it would be in the strict sense inhuman to go back on. The real divide runs through the heart of modern humanism itself, between its materialistic interpretation and its spiritual one. And it seems to me that the latter has to accept a certain reworking of its vocabulary and with it of the message of the Christian religion. I see at least five arguments that plead in favor of such a reworking of religion.

The positing, on the very basis of humanism itself (that is, in full agreement with the refusal of arguments from authority), of forms of transcendence in every area of life, thought, and culture. We continue, without even being aware of it, to posit values higher than mere existence, values for which, at the very least, it is worth risking our lives. Love, to be sure, is the most visible and strongest of these values, not only because it becomes incarnate in relation to other people, but because it gives life to all the other orders as well—from law to ethics, by way of art, culture, and science. We can love another human being, but we can also love justice, beauty, and truth. We live in peaceful, pacified societies, nourished on life-enhancing ideologies, which tend to make us believe that risk is the greatest evil. Better red than dead, it was said, and this slogan took on an exemplary value. But instead it conceals the fact that we live permanently with this risk and that without it life would not be worth living. If there did not exist beings or values for which I would in some way be ready to risk my life, I would not amount to much of a person. It would be to admit that I did not love. We may forget this at times, but it is difficult always to deny it. This is also why an attachment to values radically transcends the world of mere objects, because they are of another order, implying a resistance to materialism, and finally an aspiration to a genuine *spirituality.* "Finally," because today it is on a human basis that such a spirituality can reestablish the religious category of a beyond in human life. Subsequent, not prior, to our conscience, as the principles of moral theology would have it. Transcendence in self-immanence, therefore, but nonetheless radical transcendence in regard to materialism.

From this follows a second analogy with religion: not only does transcendental humanism posit values beyond life, it does so by recourse to a demonstration held to ground this gesture in reason. This means that these values preserve an unavoidable element of mystery, in spite of their being rooted in our human conscience rather than in some authoritarian revelation. From Descartes to Husserl by way of Kant, the philosophical tradition to which I link this transcendental humanism has never stopped positing "extra-worldly" values and meanings. Whether we designate them as "innate ideas," "eternal truths," "a priori categories," or "existentials" doesn't really matter here. In each of these cases it is a matter of unveiling a radical transcendence in relation to the "ontic" sphere of ordinary nature. We can attempt to justify and argue for this assertion, but it is not in the strict sense demonstrable. The experiences it is grounded on are inner ones and finally come down to a simple "rigorous" but never "exact" phenomenological "showing." This makes them a privileged target for those forms of reductionism determined to get as quickly as possible, based on an unshakable chain of reasoning, to an assumed origin either in nature or in history. An absolute relativism is supposed to follow, but this is not the case. Two plus two continues to make four for everyone, at every time and place, and this proposition—the simplest of all—nevertheless remains an absolute enigma. "What is incomprehensible," said Einstein, "is that the world should be comprehensible," evidence that a sense of mystery is not foreign to the scientific mind, provided it is genuinely scientific. In the supposedly more subjective order of ethics, some values do accede in an irresistible way to this same universality: for example, without having to look far, those of the Declaration of the Rights of Man, for which even fundamentalist Muslims claim to find an equivalent in the shari'a, thereby rending an involuntary homage to it. Even the sphere of taste, the most personal of all, extends to a certain form of *common sense.* However visible these kinds of transcendence may be to each of us, they nevertheless remain surrounded by a mystery that transcendental humanism has to accept.[4] Without this mystery, not only would these kinds of transcendence evaporate but, at the same time, so would humanity as such, reduced to being a simple natural mechanism—the principle of reason. It is not by chance that different kinds of reductionism, with biologism at their head, always affirm the continuity between human beings and other animals. One tiny chromosome, they exclaim—that's the only difference! Their arguments are overwhelming and supported by the facts, to a point where we almost forget what is at issue: the reduction of human existence to nature, assimilating it to one form of life among others.

A third analogy with religion: These kinds of transcendence, incarnated in the immanence of a conscience forever mysterious to itself, *connect* human beings to one another. Positing extraworldly values, whether they occur in the order of science, ethics, or art, defines the *community* of human persons, whereas inscribing values in the world separates them. Transcendental humanism is therefore an abstract humanism in the sense this term possesses in the Declaration of the Rights of Man. Rights do not reside in communal ties; they are inherent in the humanity of human beings as such, in abstraction from any particular roots. Thus it is universal values that will henceforth be called on to bind us together instead of individual attachments, which always run the risk, if they are misunderstood, of dividing us. Transcendental humanism thus preserves from religion the idea of a communal bond among human beings. But simply speaking, this bond no longer is situated in a tradition, in a heritage imposed from the outside, in something that comes before human conscience but is subsequent to it in what we must henceforth think of as something that can be the modern analogue of lost traditions: a posttraditional identity.

If we add that the kinds of transcendence so posited in a mode we can call nondogmatic are, as such, *highly valued* by human beings, we can indeed subsume them under the category of the *sacred*, as the reason sacrifices are possible. It is by positing extraworldly values that human beings show themselves to be truly human, distinct from the mechanisms of the natural and animal universe to which the different forms of reductionism constantly are trying to limit us. If the sacred is no longer rooted in a tradition whose legitimacy would be linked to a revelation prior to conscience, we must henceforth situate it in the human heart. This is why transcendental humanism is a humanism of man made god. If human beings were not in some way gods, they would no longer be human beings. We have to presuppose in them something of the sacred or accept their reduction to mere animality.

These are mysterious, sacred kinds of transcendence that bind us together because they aim at the universal, but also at a relation to eternity, even to immortality. To think of ourselves as justified, as *reasonable* in risking our lives for another being or for values, means, if we think about it, relating ourselves to something beyond time. For a finite being, conscious of its mortality, it means positing something more valuable than life and thereby beyond it. This is the ultimate paradox of this humanism of man made god, since it is from within a temporality in which we are wholly submerged that we sense ourselves to be required to act by something outside ourselves that we are totally ignorant about apart from the demand it makes on us.

This humanism will upset traditional Christians, who will see sacrilege and idolatry in the movement of humanizing the divine. But this divinization of the human will also give rise to mistrust and irony on the part of the materialists. They will discern in this new kind of spiritualism a supplementary avatar of idealism, one that can be quickly dealt with by the further pursuit of science or critical thinking. To the former, I would like to recall the words Christ addressed to the Jews who were getting ready to stone him. "I have shown you many good works from the Father. For which of these are you going to stone me?" The Jews answered, "It is not for a good work that we are going to stone you, but for blasphemy, because you, though only a human being, are making yourself God." Jesus answered, "Is it not written in your law, 'I said, you are gods?'" (John 10:32–34).

To the latter I will say only that the project of revealing the "natural grounds of ethics," of knowledge, and of the arts, so typical today in some currents of modern biology, risks turning into a trap. Please understand me: just as I respect faith, even in its traditional forms, I feel no unease with regard to "scientific" attempts to lay bare the natural or historical origin of values. It is just that the project seems to me to be affected by an inaugural vice, if I can put it this way, as soon as it claims to be exhaustive. If we admit that we can get to the point of identifying some "neuronal basis" underlying our capacity to make ethical or aesthetic choices, why should we assume that science can go so far as to make sense of these choices themselves as rational? Does anyone seriously think we might one day explain the commitments of an individual to or against racism, democracy, the equality of the sexes, and so on by anatomical or genetic differences? The difference between a German who chooses to be a Nazi and another one, perhaps in the same family, who joins the resistance will never be explained by biology, at least not except, in a surprising reversal, through a confirmation of Nazi ideology itself. Yet this kind of difference did in fact exist. The real divergences, those that on the level of values truly count, are infinitesimal and imperceptible to the gaze of the heavy machinery that makes up reductionism.

We come to, I think, the greatest paradox of our secular relationship to Christianity. The birth of modern emotional life, the affective ground of the most precious human relations, was tied to leaving behind a religion that claimed to deliver a message of love. This was what gave significance and vitality to the communitarianism of an earlier day. As a result, it is what had first to be opposed in order to get beyond the logic of the "marriage of convenience." Today the church tries to fight against this loss of the traditional relationship to revelation. It takes a stand against the overly proud demands for the freedom of conscience and of "thinking for yourself." This is a call to get back into line again that seems doomed to fail, for reasons of principle. Not that it won't find an echo among those—and they are numerous—who would like finally to rediscover some *indubitable* landmarks, solid truths, sure to calm the fears that arise in all of us owing to contemporary life. The extraordinary media-oriented success of the pope's tours bears witness to this. But the refusal of arguments from authority is not a sudden turn of fortune, an accidental decline in response to which we just need to pull ourselves together. It was an event history made use of to reveal human beings to themselves. For once unanimous, when it comes to this topic philosophy from Descartes to Hegel has irreversibly carried the day over the claims of any dogmatic religion. Human beings are human only in that they are free, and heteronomy tends toward reification. A restoration of the *form* of religion, that of an inherited tradition, will thus run into obstacles that do not have to do with a simple struggle against an allegedly historical decline.

What is applicable today about the *content* of the Gospels, on the other hand, is striking. Whereas religions of law seem always to be in decline or drawn to the temptations of fundamentalism, that of love can be reconciled with the motivations that the historians of *mentalités* have revealed to us. *Philia* is what takes us beyond the Christian religion, but it is also what makes this religion meaningful and nourishes *agape* in an unexpected way. In the past, people were attached to the religious *form* as such, but its content, its message of love, was hardly supported by the reality of human relations. Modern people, on the contrary, reject the heteronomy of theological ethics yet see introduced into their everyday life feelings likely to instantiate the *content* of a discourse that sacralizes love and makes it the central location for the meaning of life. This paradox is experienced concretely by a good number of Christians. Sometimes they feel closer to an atheistic philosophy preaching the beauty of *agape* than to a head of the church concerned to restore a bygone splendor.

In this way modern humanism, without even thinking about it, links up again with one central theme of Christianity. Love is, par excellence, the feeling that gives life, breath, and soul to a "personal structure of meaning." The other side of the coin is that mourning is not merely psychological suffering but, above all else, the test of nonmeaning. The world becomes empty, it no longer has anything to say, it no longer *means* or *wants* to say anything— this is a type of anxiety that believers can escape only by positing an absolute subject. God is love and, happily, infinite. He cannot die or, as a result, fail to give some sign of himself. Nonmeaning is banished forever. Modern humanism recognizes itself in one aspect of this message, if not in all of it. For it too love is the privileged site of meaning, and it is through love alone that the religious tenor of sacrifice perpetuates itself. But a divinized humanity has taken the place of the absolute subject. It is what I have to think of as eternal, as what must not disappear if meaning is to exist on the face of this earth. This is the significance of Hans Jonas's much discussed call for a "principle of responsibility" where it comes down to us to preserve for future generations at any price the conditions for an existence worthy of this name. This is why the nuclear danger has such a specific gravity for the collective imagination. It symbolizes the previously inconceivable possibility of an instantaneous liquidation of all human life. Because it represents a maximal power of annihilation, it makes us turn to that within ourselves that can respond to it. *Sublime* responsibility, in the literal sense of the word—superior to this power and transcending it. Just as it draws on the ideal of Christian love, modern humanism agrees with it about the meaning of hell: solitude within a universe completely deprived of meaning. Absolute evil remains attached to the idea of an irremediable *separation* from the divine, an eternal lack of love, and thus of meaning. The devil's well-known temptations have no other end in sight. He is, by the very etymology of his name, the one who separates. Even when humanized, his figure still continues to be present and, negatively, to give meaning to our existence.

We are living today, I believe, at a moment where the two processes I have attempted to describe in this book—the humanization of the divine and the divinization of the human—intersect. This intersection is a point, and this point is one of *confusion*—how could it be otherwise? I am well aware that this lack of exactness will upset some. The materialists, because the acknowledgment of transcendence escapes the logic of science and of genealogy. Surely Christians, because it constrains them to reformulate their beliefs in terms that must be finally compatible with the rejection of all arguments from authority. But if the divine is not of a material order, if its "existence" is not in space and time, it is in the hearts of human beings that it must henceforth be situated, as well as in those kinds of transcendence that they perceive, in themselves, as both belonging to them and always escaping them.

NOTES

Introduction

1. Sogyal Rinpoche, *The Tibetan Book of Living and Dying* (San Francisco: Harper San Francisco, 1992), 28.

2. Because it refuses the idea of a transcendent God, Buddhism is sometimes considered not to be a religion. The point is debatable. In any case, it does constitute a spiritual tradition that seeks to take up the ultimate questions of human life.

3. It is from this point of view that Jean Paul II, in his encyclical *The Gospel of Life*, condemns euthanasia and even goes so far as to praise the suffering that precedes death. John Paul II, *The Encyclicals in Everyday Language*, ed. Joseph G. Donders (Maryknoll, N.Y.: Orbis, 1996), 251.

4. John Paul II, *Gospel of Life*, 274.

5. Jean-Jacques Rousseau, *Discourse on Inequality*, in *"The First and Second Discourses" Together with the Replies to Critics and "Essay on the Origin of Languages,"* trans. Victor Gourevitch (New York: Harper and Row, 1986), 148–50.

6. Heidegger often described these paradoxes of everydayness. In the world of modern work, each action serves another action, which in turn serves another, with no final term ever giving meaning to the process. When we are caught up in this chain of utilities, without thinking about it, we "function" well. Everything, after all, runs. But sometimes a kind of boredom seizes us, which leads to anxiety. See, for example, his *What*

Is Metaphysics? Sartre's concept of "nausea" is based in large part on this analysis.

7. See François Furet, *The Passing of an Illusion: The Idea of Communism in the Twentieth Century,* trans. Deborah Furet (Chicago: University of Chicago Press, 1999).

8. André Comte-Sponville, "Sagesse et désespoir," in *Une éducation philosophique* (Paris: PUF, 1989), 352.

9. Cited in ibid., 349.

10. Dalai Lama, *La voie de la liberté* (Paris: Calmann-Lévy, 1995), 67.

11. "Buddhist practice teaches us not to ignore misfortunes but to recognize them and confront them by preparing ourselves straightaway so that in the moment of experiencing them, our suffering is not completely intolerable. . . . Strive, through your spiritual practice, to detach yourself from the objects of attachment" (ibid., 68). Other Buddhists insist even more strongly than the Dalai Lama that the struggle against attachment leads not to detachment, to indifference, but rather to a "nonattachment" that does not exclude the joy of living. See Rinpoche, *Tibetan Book of Living and Dying,* 35.

12. "In being so preoccupied with this life, we tend to work for those we love most—our kin and our friends—and to try to ensure that they are happy. If others try to harm them, we immediately assign them the label 'enemies,' with the result that illusions such as desire and hate grow like a river during the spring floods" (*Voie de la liberté,* 68). Only the monastic life allows us to avoid these vulnerabilities to which love and friendship inevitably expose us (ibid., 149, 143).

13. Ibid., 69.

14. Ibid., 70.

15. Ibid., 72. "The consciousness of death is the cornerstone of the Way. Before we come to this full consciousness, all the other stones remain hindrances" (82).

16. Ibid., 143.

17. "In the same manner, we wrongly believe that the body and the mind possess a kind of self—from there flows every other lure, such as desire and anger. Because of this egoistical attitude, this misunderstanding of ourselves, we make a distinction between self and others. Then, as a function of the way others treat us, we love some of them to whom we attach ourselves, and we consider others as more distant, putting them among our enemies. Then we experience anger and hate" (ibid., 144).

18. Ibid., 47.

19. Comte-Sponville, *Éducation philosophique,* 53.

20. As the books of André Comte-Sponville demonstrate.

21. André Comte-Sponville himself is not the target of the following objections. In *Valeurs et vérité: Études cyniques* (Paris: PUF, 1994), he invites us to distinguish different orders of the real, so that one cannot reduce the "moral" sphere (of the imperative law) to the spiritual, the "ethical" (which is that of love). The whole problem posed by this distinction of orders, of course, is to avoid having a higher order make a lower one appear "illusory." For one might then assign to philosophy, as a quest for wisdom, the goal of elevating us to the highest sphere in doing without the others. It is then, but only then, that such a mysticism of love stops being human and falls, it seems to me, under the objections I am about to formulate.

22. This also applies to the sympathy that surrounds those forms of spirituality said to be less "authoritarian" than that defended today by the Catholic Church. In interviewing the Dalai Lama, Jean-Claude Carrière was happy to discover in him a vision of the world "that in no way requires us to adhere to some dogmatism," even when it was a question of his most traditional and least challenged pillars, such as the notion of reincarnation. "Here is what the Dalai Lama told me: 'For us Orientals, reincarnation is something like a fact. But if science can demonstrate to us that it is nothing, that it has no basis, then we must abandon it!' Here again, rather than providing an answer based on divine revelation, Buddhism leaves the question open, in suspense. The same goes for the existence of God. One doesn't deny his existence, but neither does one affirm it. One can take it for granted if it allows for the real work that consists in seeking the truth in itself, of making one's own way" (*L'Express*, 25 May 1995). In short, religion à la carte. Religion, may I be allowed to say, that seems to me to fit better with the spirit of our times—materialist and libertarian—than with the canonical texts. It is not easy to grasp, for example, how a doctrine that means to distance you in the first place and above all else from the illusions of the "self" can come back to this as the ultimate criterion of all truth. But so what—this is how many Westerners see it, and this perception, whatever degree of distortion it may represent, is undoubtedly an indication of the demand to "think and live for oneself" so characteristic of democratic societies. In this regard the Buddhism with a human face so readily depicted for us today is a more attractive alternative figure than are the fundamentalist versions of revealed religions.

23. It is impossible here to list exhaustively all the works devoted to this question. Among recent ones, Marcel Gauchet, *The Disenchantment of the World: A Political History of Religion*, trans. Oscar Burge (Princeton: Princeton University Press, 1997), has already become a classic. As

for ethics, Gilles Lipovetsky, *Le crépuscule du devoir: L'éthique indolore des nouveaux temps démocratiques* (Paris: Gallimard, 1992), presents an interesting perspective. From Germany, there is the monumental work of Hans Blumenberg, *The Legitimacy of the Modern Age,* trans. Robert M. Wallace (Cambridge: MIT Press, 1983), which takes up and extends the older but still noteworthy analysis of Ernst Cassirer, *The Individual and the Cosmos in Renaissance Philosophy,* trans. Mario Domandi (New York: Harper and Row, 1964). For the religious background to the secular world, see Hugh Trevor-Roper, *From Counter-Reformation to Glorious Revolution* (Chicago: University of Chicago Press, 1992), and to be sure, Karl Barth, *Protestant Theology in the Nineteenth Century: Its Background and History* (Valley Forge, Pa.: Judson Press, 1973).

24. I am thinking of the way John Rawls presents his two principles of justice as a necessary choice.

25. See André Comte-Sponville, "Le capitalisme est-il moral?" in *Valeur et vérité,* 207–26.

26. See Charles Taylor, *Le malaise de la modernité* (Paris: Cerf, 1994).

27. Strictly speaking, "every postulation of a 'non-immanent actuality,' or anything which is not contained in the phenomenon, even if intended by the phenomenon, and which is therefore given in the second sense, is bracketed, i.e., suspended." Edmund Husserl, *The Idea of Phenomenology,* trans. William P. Alston and George Nakhnikian (The Hague: Martinus Nijhoff, 1964), 35. This is a new formulation of Cartesian doubt. What is absolutely certain is that I in fact have in myself states of consciousness, and these states of consciousness possess some contents. As to knowing whether these contents are "true," whether they refer to some external reality transcending my representation, for the time being all this remains problematic.

28. "Even if I raise questions about the existence and reaching the object of this relation to transcendent things, still it has something which can be grasped in the pure phenomenon. The relating-to-itself-to-transcendent-things, whether it is meant in this or that way, is still an inner feature of the phenomenon" (ibid., 36).

29. Whence the distinction proposed by Husserl between "effective immanence" and "actual immanence," which includes, in relation to the former, a certain measure of transcendence.

30. See on this point the essays on "Phenomenology and Theology," edited by Jean-Louis Chrétien, published as part 2 of Dominique Janicaud et al., *Phenomenology and the "Theological Turn": The French Debate* (New York: Fordham University Press, 2000), especially Jean-Luc Marion's "The Saturated Phenomenon," 176–216.

31. "To solicit a thought thinking more than it thinks, the Infinite cannot incarnate itself in a Desirable, cannot, being infinite, enclose itself in an end. It solicits through a face. A Thou is inserted between the I and the absolute He." Emmanuel Levinas, *Entre Nous: On Thinking-of-the-Other,* trans. Michael B. Smith and Barbara Harshav (New York: Columbia University Press, 1998), 58.

32. That Levinas hardly wished to explain himself in terms of the philosophical status of his own beliefs, that he wanted it to be his private affair, and that in this way he perhaps remains part of a traditional framework, changes nothing as regards the fact that his thought, inspired by phenomenology, may inspire us to inscribe the representation of the sacred in a humanistic framework. It is odd, given these conditions, that phenomenology so often serves—notably in the shift from Husserl to Heidegger—to reintroduce traditional attitudes and contents instead of deepening the extraordinary potential of modernity that lies at its own origin.

33. The classic thesis that the social sciences derived from romanticism needs to be reconsidered from this perspective.

34. There is nothing surprising, therefore, about the fact that it was a Cartesian, Leibniz, who both first formulated the principle of sufficient reason and theorized about the unconscious, any more than it is not surprising that, in these conditions, he should propose, starting from the principle of sufficient reason, the model of a "social unconscious" that would incorporate both Mandeville and liberal theorists of the "invisible hand" along with the individual unconscious (the "little differences"). I agree, readers will recognize, with those who say that Marcel Gauchet's *Disenchantment of the World* is one of the more important works published in France in the past ten years. It is because of this that I want to draw that author's attention to one difficulty that seems essential to me, which affects his studies devoted to the history of the unconscious and, beyond this, to modern subjectivity in general. I do not think we should, as Gauchet sometimes suggests, set in opposition three political temporalities as though they succeeded one another in history to the point of defining three epochs: the past (tradition or religion), the present (characterized by social contract theories still linked to absolutism), and the future, inaugurated by Benjamin Constant and other liberal theorists of the invisible hand or the cunning of reason. I can see how this threefold scheme allows one to found a history of subjectivity and, in particular, of the social and individual figures of the unconscious. It is clear, for example, that with liberal theories of the market, a certain idea of tradition, and with it of the social and even individual unconscious, is opposed to

the illusions of individualism inherited from the Enlightenment. But this periodizing stumbles over one *fact,* one that is both historical and philosophical. In the seventeenth century, with Leibniz, the structure of the "invisible hand," as well as that of the individual unconscious, which was to be taken up again at the beginning of the eighteenth century by Mandeville, had already appeared, long before the shock of the French Revolution. And this was so for one fundamental reason. Already with Leibniz, the two faces of modern subjectivity were connected *in one and the same movement,* that of reason and that of the will. This was the point of my work devoted to the system of philosophies of history. "Voluntarist," revolutionary theories of society as well as of the subject were contemporary with, not prior to, those of the "cunning of reason." Which is why the conflict between voluntarism and political liberalism will not cease to mark our political life, even in today's social democracy (cf. the conflict between "*blanquisme*" and "revisionism"). It is also why, from the seventeenth century on, the hypothesis of the unconscious will haunt all of modern philosophy (with Kant even representing, for the thought of a "cloven" subject, an important enough step to have drawn the notice of authors as little to be suspected of any sympathy for this tradition as Lacan). What is more, the Leibnizian conception of "tiny unconscious perceptions" will lie at the origin of a whole current of scientific, and not just philosophical, psychology—one that will be concerned, for example, with Wundt, about the crucial question of "perceptual thresholds."

35. Regarding this theme see Jacques Rollet, "Penser la foi," in *Penser la foi: Recherches en théologie aujourd'hui. Mélanges offerts à Joseph Moingt,* ed. Joseph Doré, Christoph Theobald, and Joseph Moingt (Paris: Cerf, 1992).

36. To recall the title of a work by Father Valadier (Paul Valadier, *Éloge de la conscience* [Paris: Seuil, 1994]).

CHAPTER ONE

1. As Cardinal Lustiger suggests, based on a close analysis. See the following noteworthy passage: "In the debates over ethics that seek to influence public opinion, conscience is in a way placed under the tutelage of committees on ethics or professional codes of conduct. Like legislative or regulatory measures, these decisions take the place of a moral norm. But the law does not obligate or authorize itself to conscience unless it conforms to moral reason." Jean-Marie Lustiger, *Devenez dignes de la condition humaine* (Paris: Flammarion, 1995), 20.

2. Jacques Rollet, "Les croyances des Français," *Études,* October 1995,

discusses an interesting poll carried out in 1994 by the CSA Institute. To the question, "In the big decisions of your life, do you pay more attention to your conscience or to the positions of the church?" 83 percent of the French people polled answered "my conscience," and only 1 percent said "the positions of the church" (9 percent said "both").

3. Regarding this point, see the articles appearing in *Le Débat*, no. 75 (May–August 1993). See also Jean Stoezel, *Les valeurs du temps présent: Une enquête européene* (Paris: PUF, 1983); Hélène Riffault, *Les valeurs des Français* (Paris: PUF, 1994); and the articles published in the magazine *Panorama* (November 1993) under the heading "The French, Death, and the Beyond."

4. *Splendor of Truth*, secs. 32–34, in John Paul II, *The Encyclicals in Everyday Language*, ed. Joseph G. Donders (Maryknoll, N.Y.: Orbis, 1996), 212–13.

5. Even if a few of his bishops may suggest, for those who are unable to follow this rule, that some kinds of behavior are less troublesome than others.

6. *Splendor of Truth*, sec. 36, p. 214. See also, regarding the classical question of prudence, sec. 56, pp. 221–22.

7. See also sec. 90, p. 234. On more than one point the pope's criticism of utilitarianism is similar to that of John Rawls: it is illegitimate, in the name of the general good, to sacrifice the least portion of human dignity.

8. *Catechism of the Catholic Church* (Liguori, Mo.: Liguori, 1994), sec. 2266, p. 546.

9. As was recently shown by the polemics arising from the publication in 1994 of Jacques Duquesne's *Jésus* (Paris: Flammarion, 1994).

10. As perhaps will be come clearer in what follows, that Drewermann has continued to denounce the heritage of the Enlightenment changes nothing as regards the fact that his theology belongs within the general framework of humanism.

11. Eugen Drewermann, *De la naissance des dieux à la naissance du Christ* (Paris: Seuil, 1992).

12. Jean-Pierre Bagot, *Le cas Drewermann: Les documents* (Paris: Cerf, 1993).

13. Eugen Drewermann, *La Parole qui guérit* (Paris: Cerf, 1991), 60.

14. See especially Eugen Drewermann, *La peur et la faute* (Paris: Cerf, 1992).

15. Drewermann, *De la naissance des dieux à la naissance du Christ*, 48.

16. As the following text, among others, testifies: "I believe in God in two ways. First, I believe that the natural sciences are in the process of

showing us the outlines of a new image of theological reflection. They make clear the necessity of respecting a system that is self-organizing. We can no longer talk of matter and spirit as we have habitually done in the West. We are discovering spirit to be a structural property of every complex system. Meaning arises of its own accord from the process of evolution. In this sense God is something that unfolds in the world and with the world. This quite poetic and creative idea, which recalls pantheism, is also highly insightful and leads us to rediscover in a new way our bond with all creatures. . . . A religion will henceforth no longer be credible unless it underscores the religious meaning of the bond between humanity and nature and grasps the constitutive unity of body and soul. . . . The second point is that it will no longer be possible to banish the anxiety that comes from the fact of grasping oneself as an individual. . . . I consider faith in a personal God to be an urgent postulate for responding to this human anxiety. I believe this is what Jesus thought when he undertook to give us the courage to walk on water and to feel the abyss that bears us up once we have such confidence. These two images of God, that of a personal God and that of spirit developing of its own accord, that of systematic evolution, are antithetical. But I take it as possible that the old trinitarian doctrine of Christianity is capable of uniting these two roles." *Frankfurter Allgemeine,* 3 May 1991; translated and discussed in the issue of *L'Actualité Religieuse dans le Monde* devoted entirely to Drewermann (March 1993), 58.

17. Eugen Drewermann, *Les voies du coeur* (Paris: Cerf, 1993).

18. Eugen Drewermann, *De l'immortalité des animaux* (Paris: Cerf, 1992).

19. Eugen Drewermann, *Le progrès meurtrier* (Paris: Stock, 1993).

20. On this point, see the article by Françoise Champion and Martine Cohen in *Le Débat,* May–August 1993.

21. Eugen Drewermann, *Sermons pour le temps pascal* (Paris: Michel, 1994), 94.

22. Analyzed by Jean-Luc Marion in his *Prolégomènes à la charité* (Paris: Éditions de La Différence, 1986).

23. Here, as one example, is an extract from the act of accusation issued in November 1995 against certain Serb leaders by the International Penal Tribunal for the former Yugoslavia: "Thousands of men were executed and buried in fields, hundreds of others were buried alive, men and women were mutilated before being killed, children slaughtered in front of their mothers, a grandfather forced to eat the liver of his grandson." This document is important, for it was written by professional jurists who could draw only on irrefutable testimony and evidence. It is a sign

of the breadth of these disasters that the accusation in question has to do with only a single episode: the fall of Srebrenica in July 1995.

24. As the reappearance of works devoted to it, with the blessing of high clerical officials, bears witness. We can cite, among others, Father Gabriele Armoth, the exorcist for the diocese of Rome, *An Exorcist Tells His Story* (San Francisco: Ignatius Press, 1999); Georges Morand, the chaplain of one of the large hospitals in Paris, *Sors de cet homme, Satan* (Paris: Fayard, 1993); or even Father Louis Costel, the scourge of the evil one in the diocese of Coutances, including *Le diable et l'exorciste* published in collaboration with Daniel Yonnet (Rennes: Éditions Ouest-France, 1993).

25. Among the many difficulties on the theological plane posed by the hypothesis of Satan, let us also mention the one that occupied the Italian philosopher Giovanni Papini in his well-known book on the devil: Can Christianity in preaching the love of its enemy exclude the demon from that love? I thank Nicolaus Sombart for having drawn my attention to this curious yet intelligent work (*Il diavolo;* translated by Adrienne Foulke as *The Devil* [New York: Dutton, 1954]).

26. Jean-Jacques Rousseau, *Emile, or On Education,* trans. Alan Bloom (New York: Basic Books, 1979), 282.

27. As I suggested in *The System of Philosophies of History,* the second volume of my *Political Philosophy* trans. Franklin Philip (Chicago: University of Chicago Press, 1992), there are in fact two figures for the negation of subjectivity and, in this, for that of evil: that of determinism and that, just as formidable, of deconstructions of "metaphysics." Arendt belongs to this second strain, inspired by Heidegger, when she—wrongly I believe—pleads for the idea of a banality of evil.

28. For a clear, albeit tendentious look at this well-publicized quarrel, see the article by Tim Mason that appeared in the September 1982 issue of *Le Débat* with the title "Banalisation du nazisme?"

29. Which, moreover, was functionalist. But even were it inspired by Marxism, the result would have been exactly the same. For it is the laying bare of forms of determinism that weakens the idea of responsibility and leads to dehumanizing evil.

30. Notably Karl Dietrich Bracher and Klaus Hildebrandt.

31. André Green, "Le Mal," *Nouvelle Revue de Psychanalyse,* no. 38 (autumn 1988). We could cite other examples of nonreductionist interpretations in the social sciences as well. The place Alain Touraine grants to the freedom of "actors" is well known, for example.

32. Concerning this definition of human being and a comparison with the animal realm as regards the problem of freedom, good, and evil,

see the first part of Luc Ferry, *Le nouvel ordre écologique: L'arbre, l'animal et l'homme* (Paris: Grasset, 1992).

33. Alexis Philonenko, *L'archipel de la conscience européene* (Paris: Grasset, 1990), 108ff.

CHAPTER TWO

1. See Alain-Gérard Slama, *L'angelisme exterminateur: Essai sur l'ordre morale contemporain* (Paris: Grasset, 1993).

2. What Marcel Gauchet calls "la désertion civique" of ordinary citizens.

3. Gilles Lipovetsky, *Le crépuscule du devoir: L'éthique indolore des nouveaux temps démocratiques* (Paris: Gallimard, 1992).

4. Ibid., 13.

5. Ibid., 14.

6. Ibid.

7. However, the model of love as a passion, later reworked by the romantics, does find its origin at the end of the eleventh century and beginning of the twelfth with the elaboration of courtly love. Since then, European poetry has continued to draw its inspiration from the same sources as did the troubadours. See Denis de Rougement, *Love in the Western World*, trans. Montgomery Belgion, rev. ed. (New York: Pantheon, 1956), whose theses, for all that they have been challenged, are still stimulating.

8. Philippe Ariès, *L'enfant et la vie familiale sous l'Ancien Régime* (Paris: Plon, 1960; rev. ed. Paris: Seuil, 1973). For an overall view of the wide range of work devoted to this question over the past thirty years in Europe and the United States, see the excellent clear and synthetic work of François Lebrun, *La vie conjugale sous l'Ancien Régime* (Paris: Colin, 1993).

9. This is, to be sure, a central argument for a certain feminism, best represented in France by the work of Elisabeth Badinter. The partisans of the idea of an eternal human nature have not failed to indicate their reservations about this research. See, for example, James Q. Wilson, *The Moral Sense* (New York: Free Press, 1993). As we shall see below, however, a certain number of historical facts are difficult to make sense of outside the framework of a history of *mentalités,* whatever the epistemological difficulties may be.

10. Bear in mind this double limitation—geographical and historical. Outside this exact framework the following remarks lose their credibility. They even become absurd if used, wrongly, to conclude that "love did

not appear until the eighteenth century"! On the other hand, it is interesting to consider why it was absent during the late European Middle Ages in *family* relations, particularly marriage.

11. See, for example, Edward Shorter, *The Making of the Modern Family* (New York: Basic Books, 1975).

12. "The first motivation for the lie was the desire to spare the sick person, to assume the burden of his ordeal. But this sentiment, whose origin we know (the intolerance of another's death and the confidence shown by the dying person in those about him) very rapidly was covered over by a different sentiment; a new sentiment characteristic of modernity: one must avoid—no longer for the sake of the dying person, but for society's sake, for the sake of those close to the dying person—the disturbance and the overly strong and unbearable emotion caused by the ugliness of dying and by the very presence of death in the midst of a happy life, for it is henceforth given that life is always happy or should always seem to be so." Philippe Ariès, *Western Attitudes toward Death: From the Middle Ages to the Present*, trans. Patricia M. Ranum (Baltimore: Johns Hopkins University Press, 1974), 86–87.

13. Nothing makes this clearer than what Ariès himself has to say about his research into the attitude toward death that prevailed for centuries during the Middle Ages: "First of all, we encountered a very old, very durable, very massive sentiment of familiarity with death, with neither fear nor despair, halfway between passive resignation and mystical trust. Even more than during other vigorous periods of existence, Destiny was revealed through Death, and in those days the dying person accepted it in a public ceremony whose ritual was fixed by custom. The ceremony of death was then at least as important as the ceremony of the funeral and mourning. Death was the awareness by each person of a Destiny in which his own personality was not annihilated but *put to sleep—resquies*. . . . This belief did not make as great a distinction as we today make between time before and time after, the life and the afterlife. The living and the dead in both medieval literature and in popular folk tales show the same simple and vague, yet rather racy natures. . . . This way of dying signified a surrender of oneself to Destiny and an indifference to the too-individual and diverse forms of the personality" (ibid., 103–4).

14. Shorter nicely sums up the significance of this mutation in the following brief formulation. "In the 'good' old days, people learned their identity and the place that came down to them in the eternal order of things by considering the succession of generations that had preceded them—a succession that would continue beyond them into a future concerning which one could only say that it was likely to be just like the past.

If the members of traditional societies were capable of showing themselves to be calm in the face of death, it was because, in the final analysis, they had the certitude that their name and their memory would be perpetuated through the families in their lineage. Today . . . we have ceased to be interested in our lineage as a way of cheating death and we have at the same time renounced those ties that bound one generation to another" (Shorter, *Making of the Modern Family*, 16).

15. From the first appearances of modern individualism, already in the Middle Ages, "death ceased being the forgetting of a self that was vigorous but without ambition; it ceased being the acceptance of a formidable Destiny, but one which concealed no novelty. Instead it became a place where the individual traits of each life, of each biography, appeared in the bright light of the clear conscience, a place where everything was weighed, counted, and written down, where everything could be changed, lost, or saved" (ibid., 104–5).

16. Lebrun, *Vie conjugale*.

17. See Jean-Louis Flandrin, *Families in Former Times: Kinship, Household, and Sexuality*, trans. Richard Southern (New York: Cambridge University Press, 1979), 132.

18. Ibid., 95.

19. "The physical matrix within which the traditional family found itself discouraged intimacy. Too many curious faces thrust themselves into *la vie intime;* too many heterogeneous elements swirled through the household. The community's informal surveillance was omnipresent, thanks to the arrangement of space, and the formal restrictions that the social authorities placed on sentiment, and inclination was too powerful to let close emotional ties arise" (Shorter, *Making of the Modern Family*, 53).

20. We should note that this "potentiality" changes meaning depending on whether the dimension of time valued by society is that of the past (as in traditional societies) or the future (as in modern societies). For us, as heirs of Rousseau who assign to human existence an ideal of "perfectibility," a child is filled with hope and promise. For people of the past, he was above all incomplete, hence imperfect, and since his vocation was essentially to repeat some already existing model, any hope placed in him was strictly limited.

21. Flandrin, *Families*, 137.

22. Ibid., 153.

23. Shorter, *Making of the Modern Family*, 176. This practice, contrary to what we might think, was not carried out only by the poorest families. Shorter cites the "typical" example of a master weaver who,

when questioned by a friend about a sister-in-law who was said to have abandoned her second child even though she had plenty of funds to live on and was said to be an "upstanding woman," replied, "Well, yes she is . . . but her child got in the way of her daily routines and moreover, she exposed her first as well" (175). Let us also note how Shorter, in agreement with other historians, but also with the most enlightened testimony of the period, describes wet nurses. "They as a rule were indifferent beyond belief to the welfare of the babies they took in. Children were commodities for them, just as, let us say, cocoa futures are commodities for a modern trader" (185). This is followed by an enumeration of the ill treatments that so often led to death.

24. However, François Lebrun cites the famous case of Rousseau, who declared himself to be convinced that his children, sent to wet nurses, had had a better education than he did. It does appear, though, that although the mortality rate was not known in detail as it is today, parents of the day were aware that to place their child with a wet nurse was to put its life in danger (Lebrun, *Vie conjugale*).

25. John Boswell, *The Kindness of Strangers: The Abandonment of Children in Western Europe from Late Antiquity to the Renaissance* (New York: Pantheon, 1988). From his side, Shorter cites, for the middle of the nineteenth century, the figure of 33,000 abandoned children in France each year, of which at least 5,000 were abandoned by their legitimate parents (*Making of the Modern Family*, 216).

26. See the figures gathered by Lebrun, *Vie conjugale*, 158ff.

27. Lebrun, *Vie conjugale*.

28. From their perspective, sociologists like Niklas Luhmann have sought to avoid the trap of causal explanations by considering the way these historical mutations were experienced in literature and translated in terms of its "semantic codes." His analyses nonetheless converge with those of Shorter as a diagnosis of the advent, so characteristic of modernity, of a private sphere where love, separated from the communitarian and economic aspects that had formerly encompassed it, became an end in itself for individuals. See Niklas Luhmann, *Love as Passion: The Codification of Intimacy*, trans. Jeremy Gaines and Doris L. Jones (Cambridge: Harvard University Press, 1986). A better rendering of the title—which is overly literal both in English and in French (*Amour comme passion*), and moreover almost unintelligible—would have been *Love-Passion* (*L'amour-passion*).

29. My remarks have often been inspired by those of Tzvetan Todorov in his *Frêle bonheur: Essai sur Rousseau* (Paris: Hachette, 1985).

30. This question arises in analogous terms in the sphere of aesthetics

in general. Today, what gives feeling a privilege above that of any other criterion of the beautiful; the problem of the objectivity of taste; and so forth.

31. In 1938 Denis de Rougemont had already devoted impressively lucid pages to this question in his *Love in the Western World,* trans. Montgomery Belgion, rev. ed. (New York: Pantheon, 1956).

32. See Eugen Drewermann, *La peur et la faute* (Paris: Cerf, 1992), 79ff.

33. For example, "Whoever comes to me, yet prefers his father, his mother," etc.

34. "Those who say, 'I love God,' and hate their brothers or sisters, are liars; for those who do not love a brother or sister whom they have seen, cannot love God whom they have not seen" (1 John 4:20).

35. Simone Weil, *Gravity and Grace,* trans. Arthur Wills (New York: Putnam's, 1952), 45.

36. Historians of *mentalités* have noted, in this regard, how the High Middle Ages seem closer to us than do the three centuries preceding the French Revolution. We need to be on guard against retrospective illusions, however. Courtly love does not really resemble "our" modern passionate love ever since its reinterpretation by the romantics. Its original meaning, which was essentially religious, is barely discernible to us today. See Rougemont, *Love in the Western World.*

37. A perfect analogy between feeling and sensation can be established. As Hegel suggests in his dialectic of "sensible certainty," it is through the impossibility of maintaining an equality between subject and object that this figure of consciousness first posits the object as essential and itself as accidental. On the philosophical level of a theory of knowledge, this position corresponds to "realism." The object exists independent of the sensation, which is pure passivity, mere reflection, of which the object is the cause.

38. Recall the well-known passage from Stendhal's *De l'amour:* "In the salt mines of Salzburg a bough stripped of its leaves by winter is thrown into the depths of the disused workings; two or three months later it is pulled out again, covered with sparkling crystals. even the tiniest twigs, no bigger than a tomtit's claw, are spangled with a vast number of shimmering, glittering diamonds, so that the original bough is no longer recognizable." Stendhal [Henri Marie Beyle], *On Love,* trans. H. B. V. under the direction of K. Scott-Moncrieff (n.p.: Boni and Liveright, 1927; Universal Library, 1967), 6. This is how the lover clothes the beloved.

39. Molière, *Don Juan,* act 1, scene 2.

40. Ibid.

41. Here I follow the commentary given by André Comte-Sponville in his *Petit traité des grandes vertus* (Paris: PUF, 1995).

42. André Comte-Sponville proposes this definition of *philia* in his *Petit traité des grandes vertus,* which I gladly accept: "I love you: I am happy that you exist. . . . *Philia* is love when it blossoms among humans, and whatever form it may take, it does not reduce to a lack and passion (to *eros*). The word therefore has a narrower extension than does the French *amour* (which can apply as well to an object, an animal, or a god), but a broader one than does our *amitié* (which is hardly ever applied, for example, between parents and children). Let us say that it is joyous love [*l'amour-joie*] inasmuch as it is reciprocal or can be so. It is the joy of loving and of being loved. . . . In short, it is active love [*l'amour-action*], which we can thereby oppose to *eros* (love as passion [*l'amour-passion*]), even if nothing prevents their convergence or going hand in hand" (330, 334–35).

43. Parodying one of Sartre's expressions, we could say that God for Simone Weil "makes himself a lack of being so that being may be." God who is infinite and perfect renounces his absolute power in order that the world and human beings can exist. It is in terms of this theory of creation that we should understand the idea, so dear to Weil, of a "weak God."

44. Comte-Sponville, *Petit traité des grandes vertus,* 364–65.

CHAPTER THREE

1. Which did not prevent a number of humanitarians from discovering their vocation by way of a commitment to the Third World. However, for this to happen required a real *aggiornamento* on their part.

2. Luc Boltanski, *La souffrance à distance* (Paris: Métailié, 1993), 247ff., gives a good analysis of the impact of the immense literature, inspired by Marxism and by Nietzsche, devoted during the seventies to the critique of philanthropy as a concealed form of domination.

3. Friedrich Nietzsche, *The Will to Power,* trans. Walter Kaufmann and R. J. Hollindale, ed. Walter Kaufmann (New York: Vintage Books, 1967), 142.

4. It is this suspicion that justifies the most radical criticisms, and this distinction (between the truth of a project and its ideological uses) that limits its impact. On this point, see Bernard-Henri Lévy, *La pureté dangereuse* (Paris: Grasset, 1994), 141ff.

5. Although *Le Monde* did report on it in its edition of 4 April 1995.

6. Not only is there nothing impossible about such a hypothesis, it

even seems quite easy to realize. It would only require having the embryos of two sisters be born at different times, keeping the second one long enough so that it could be implanted in the first!

7. See, for example, Pierre Boissier, *Henri Dunant* (Geneva: Henry Dunant Institute, 1991), a publication of the Henry Dunant Institute, whose members gave me a warm welcome for which I want here to thank them. As for the history of modern humanitarian action, see the works of Jean-Christophe Ruffin, especially *L'aventure humanitaire* (Paris: Gallimard, 1994). I want also to express my thanks to Bernard Kouchner for the time he gave me.

8. Quoted by Pierre Coissier, from whom I draw this story.

9. "Do not let happen to others . . . " Invited by the Académie Universelle des Cultures to give a lecture on "the duty of assistance," I took the occasion to discuss with Robert Badinter some ideas about the topic of my talk. It was he who suggested this formula to me in order to underscore the "plus" of universality that modern humanitarianism claims to introduce in relation to traditional forms of charity.

10. Ruffin, *Aventure humanitaire*, 50.

11. Pascal Bruckner, *La tentation de l'innocence* (Paris: Grasset, 1995).

12. Subsequent to this, Security Council resolution 688 of 5 April 1991, at the end of the Gulf War, ordered the government in Baghdad to allow humanitarian organizations to help the Kurds. Others followed: 743 (21 February 1992), creating the United Nations Protective Force, charged to oversee the application of the cease-fire of Geneva (November 1991) and of Sarajevo (January 1992); 770 (14 August 1992), intended to "open the way to humanitarian aid wherever it is necessary in Bosnia-Herzegovina"; 794 (3 December 1992), calling for the "urgent necessity to rapidly make possible humanitarian assistance throughout" Somalia; and so on.

13. Alain Destexhe, *L'humanitaire impossible* (Paris: Armand Colin, 1993). Clearly this is a book worth reading.

14. I have made my own test, and here is how it goes. Read the fifteen or twenty most recent works devoted to the misdeeds of a media-based society. The list is impressive, and one can well believe that television has taken the place of the devil himself. Consider, for example, what I found during my dip into this antimedia material, without any addition or exaggeration: television alienates minds, it shows the same thing to everyone, presenting the ideology of those who shape it; it distorts children's imaginations, impoverishes the curiosity of adults, puts the mind to sleep; it is an instrument of political control, it engineers how we think, manipulates information, imposes dominant, not to say bourgeois cultural models,

overlooking urban reality, the middle classes, low-paid work, rural life, the world of the worker; it marginalizes regional cultures and languages, engenders passivity, destroys interpersonal relations in families, kills off the book and any "difficult" culture, incites to violence and to vulgarity as well as to pornography, prevents youth from becoming adults; it competes in an unfair way with live theater, the circus, cabarets, and movies, generates indifference and apathy among citizens stuffed with useless information, abolishes cultural hierarchies, replaces information with communication, reflection with emotion, intellectual distance with the presence of volatile and superficial emotions, undervalues school; and so on and so on. We may well ask how such a monster can benefit from the complicity of the civil authorities, not to speak of the people themselves. We may well ask how, every evening, the vast majority of people gets divided between those in front of their screens and those who, even while criticizing it, can only think of how they can most quickly join them.

15. This critique is eloquently developed by Régis Debray in his *L'État séducteur* (Paris: Gallimard, 1993).

16. Who to be sure, because they have to get a "scoop," will go so far as to pride themselves on receiving on their platform or welcoming to their columns the most supposedly "non-media-centered" personalities. Thus *Paris-Match,* beneath a large (and excellent) photo of Le Clézio, had the following headline regarding the appearance of his latest book: "This voluntary exile, who avoids the press, talks exclusively with PPDA for TF1 and *Paris-Match*" (*sic*)—which for someone identified as being against the media and recognized as such by them is not so bad! One can easily cite examples like this that, beyond the anecdotal, pose the crucial problem of the status of media-oriented criticism of the media.

17. Regarding these internal polemics, and more generally the history of modern humanitarian movements, see the excellent book by Olivier Weber, *French Doctors* (Paris: Laffont, 1995).

18. See Xavier Emmanuelli, *Les prédateurs de l'action humanitaire* (Paris: Michel, 1991).

19. See *Le Monde,* 16 April 1994.

20. "If mortals succeeded in endowing their works, deeds, and words with some permanence and in arresting their perishability, then these things would, to a degree at least, enter and be at home in the world of everlastingness, and the mortals themselves would find their place in the cosmos, where everything is immortal except men." Hannah Arendt, "The Concept of History: Ancient and Modern," in Hannah Arendt, *Between Past and Future* (New York: Viking Press, 1961), 43.

21. Milan Kundera, *La lenteur* (Paris: Gallimard, 1995), 20.

22. Hans Jonas, *The Imperative of Responsibility: In Search of an Ethics for the Technological Age* (Chicago: University of Chicago Press, 1984), 134. However, I do not share Jonas's claim to demonstrate the "ontological" character of the duty of responsibility owed to a child.

23. On this point, see the analyses of Rony Brauman in his *Le crime humanitaire: Somalie* ([Paris]: Arléa, 1993).

24. As Mario Bettati has often pointed out.

25. Cf. the point made by Mario Bettati in his essay "Action humanitaire d'état et diplomatie," which appeared in a special issue of *Economica* (1993) devoted to "les relations internationales à l'épreuve de la science politique."

26. Claude Malhuret and Xavier Emmanuelli have undertaken to exercise this representation at the highest level, thereby showing that their criticism of "humanitarian politics" is confined within certain limits.

27. Roger Job, ed., *Lettres sans frontières* (Paris: Éditions Complexe, 1994).

28. Of course this is not what Rony Brauman has in mind, but the problem of meaning can be expanded in this way.

29. Aristotle, *Nicomachean Ethics,* 1120b.

30. This is the thesis defended by Francis Fukuyama, but also, in another fashion, by Pascal Bruckner in his *La mélancolie démocratique* (Paris: Seuil, 1990).

31. Depending on whether one is more "liberal" or more "faithful" to the promises of a hard, pure left, one may see in this a salutary, pedagogical effect or a betrayal.

32. CAC 40: Forty stocks tracked by the Compagnie des Agents de Change—the French equivalent of the Dow-Jones average [trans.].

33. RMI: *revenu minimum d'insertion*—a program of income support [trans.].

34. For anyone who may still doubt this, I will just recall the following extract from a speech Jack Lane gave at Blois in 1990 at a festival appropriately called "Making a Fuss": "Today, the center is the periphery. It is no longer this old town center, surveyed and listed as a national heritage. Real life is in the suburbs, with their 'integrated development zones' and their 'priority development areas,' which are often poor, to be sure, but so warm, so convivial, so colorful."

35. As the new "communitarians" have seen, Charles Taylor at their head.

36. Throughout the world, if not in France. Rawls is the living author whose work has given rise to the most discussion, to the point that a

bibliography of works about him would today form a volume of nearly eight hundred pages!

37. See Marek Halter, *La force du bien* (Paris: Laffont, 1995).

Conclusion

1. Cardinal Lustiger has clearly stated the terms of this dilemma: "The ground of positive law reveals itself to be both within and beyond itself. Civil law remains the one recognized procedure for arbitrating among opinions in democratic, pluralistic societies. Yet any regime that claims not to need or to do without an ungrounded ground of law is, hypothetically, a totalitarian one. One key to the law and to respect for liberty consists in the distance between moral obligation and its determination by the law. Yet beyond such juridical arrangements remains the instance that verifies them, the truth that grounds them. And rightly so." Jean-Marie Lustiger, *Devenez dignes de la condition humaine* (Paris: Flammarion, 1995), 36–37.

2. Friedrich Nietzsche, *Twilight of the Idols,* in *The Portable Nietzsche,* ed. and trans. Walter Kaufmann (New York: Viking, 1968), 474.

3. See my *Political Philosophy,* vol. 2, *The System of Philosophies of History,* trans. Franklin Philip (Chicago: University of Chicago Press, 1992).

4. Oddly, commentators have not paid much attention (a euphemism) to the passage in Kant's *Critique of Pure Reason* (sec. 21) where he speaks of mystery, that is, of the radical contingency at the heart of the transcendental sphere: "This peculiarity of our understanding, that it can produce a prior unity of apperception solely by means of the categories, and only by such and so many, is as little capable of further explanation as why we have just these and no other functions of judgment, or why space and time are the only forms of our possible intuition." In other words, the a priori, whose two major characteristics are universality and necessity, is at bottom thoroughly enigmatic, not to say wholly contingent.

WORKS CITED

Arendt, Hannah. *Between Past and Future.* New York: Viking, 1961.

Ariès, Phillipe. *L'enfant et la vie familiale sous l'Ancien Régime.* Paris: Plon, 1960; rev. ed. Paris: Seuil, 1973.

————. *Western Attitudes toward Death: From the Middle Ages to the Present.* Trans. Patricia M. Ranum. Baltimore: Johns Hopkins University Press, 1974.

Armoth, Gabriele. *An Exorcist Tells His Story.* San Francisco: Ignatius Press, 1999.

Bagot, Jean-Pierre. *Le cas Drewermann: Les documents.* Paris: Cerf, 1993.

Barth, Karl. *Protestant Theology in the Nineteenth Century: Its Background and History.* Valley Forge, Pa.: Judson Press, 1973.

Bettati, Mario. "Action humanitaire d'état et diplomatie." *Economica,* special issue, 1993.

Blumenberg, Hans. *The Legitimacy of the Modern Age.* Trans. Robert M. Wallace. Cambridge: MIT Press, 1983.

Boissier, Pierre. *Henri Dunant.* Geneva: Henry Dunant Institute, 1991.

Boltanski, Luc. *La souffrance à distance.* Paris: Métailié, 1993.

Boswell, John. *The Kindness of Strangers: The Abandonment of Children in Western Europe from Late Antiquity to the Renaissance.* New York: Pantheon, 1988.

Brauman, Rony. *Le crime humanitaire: Somalie.* [Paris]: Arléa, 1993.

Bruckner, Pascal. *La mélancolie démocratique.* Paris: Seuil, 1990.

————. *La tentation de l'innocence.* Paris: Grasset, 1995.

Carrière, Jean-Claude. Interview with the Dalai Lama. *L'Express,* 25 May 1995.

Cassirer, Ernst. *The Individual and the Cosmos in Renaissance Philosophy.* Trans. Mario Domandi. New York: Harper and Row, 1964.

Catechism of the Catholic Church. Liguroi, Mo.: Liguoroi, 1994.

Comte-Sponville, André. *Une éducation philosophique.* Paris: PUF, 1989.

————. *Petit traité des grandes vertus.* Paris: PUF, 1995.

————. *Valeurs et vérité: Études cyniques.* Paris: PUF, 1994.

Dalai Lama. *La voie de la liberté.* Paris: Calmann-Lévy, 1995.

Debray, Régis. *L'État séducteur.* Paris: Gallimard, 1993.

Destexhe, Alain. *L'humanitaire impossible.* Paris: Armand-Colin, 1993.

Doré, Joseph, Christoph Theobald, and Joseph Moingt, eds. *Penser la foi: Recherches en théologie aujourd'hui. Mélanges offerts à Joseph Moingt.* Paris: Cerf, 1992.

Drewermann, Eugen. *De la naissance des dieux à la naissance du Christ.* Paris: Seuil, 1992.

————. *De l'immortalité des animaux.* Paris: Cerf, 1992.

————. *La Parole qui guérit.* Paris: Cerf, 1991.

————. *La peur et la faute.* Paris: Cerf, 1992.

————. *Le progrès meurtrier.* Paris: Stock, 1993.

————. *Sermons pour le temps pascal.* Paris: Michel, 1994.

————. *Les voies du coeur.* Paris: Cerf, 1993.

Duquesne, Jacques. *Jésus.* Paris: Flammarion, 1994.

Emmanuelli, Xavier. *Les prédateurs de l'action humanitaire.* Paris: Michel, 1991.

Erhard, Benjamin. *Apologie du diable 1795.* Caen: Centre de Philosophie Politique et Juridique de l'Université, 1989.

Ferry, Luc. *Le nouvel ordre écologique: L'arbre, l'animal et l'homme.* Paris: Grasset, 1992.

————. *Political Philosophy.* Vol. 2. *The System of Philosophies of History.* Trans. Franklin Philip. Chicago: University of Chicago Press, 1992.

Flandrin, Jean-Louis. *Families in Former Times: Kinship, Household, and Sexuality.* Trans. Richard Southern. New York: Cambridge University Press, 1979.

Furet, François. *The Passing of an Illusion: The Idea of Communism in the Twentieth Century.* Trans. Deborah Furet. Chicago: University of Chicago Press, 1999.

Gauchet, Marcel. *The Disenchantment of the World: A Political History of Religion.* Trans. Oscar Burge. Princeton: Princeton University Press, 1997.

Green, André. "Le Mal." *Nouvelle Revue de Psychanalyse,* no. 38 (autumn 1988).

Halter, Marek. *La force du bien.* Paris: Laffont, 1995.

Heidegger, Martin. *What Is Metaphysics?* In *Pathmarks,* ed. Will McNeill, trans. David Farrell Krell, 82–96. New York: Cambridge University Press, 1998.

Husserl, Edmund. *The Idea of Phenomenology.* Trans. William P. Alston and George Nakhnikian. The Hague: Martinus Nijhoff, 1964.

Janicaud, Dominique, et al. *Phenomenology and the "Theological Turn": The French Debate.* New York: Fordham University Press, 2000.

Job, Roger, ed. *Lettres sans frontières.* Paris: Éditions Complexe, 1994.

John Paul II. *The Encyclicals in Everyday Language.* Ed. Joseph G. Donders. Maryknoll, N.Y.: Orbis, 1996.

Jonas, Hans. *The Imperative of Responsibility: In Search of an Ethics for the Technological Age.* Chicago: University of Chicago Press, 1984.

Kundera, Milan. *Le lenteur.* Paris: Gallimard, 1995.

Lebrun, François. *La vie conjugale sous l'Ancien Régime.* Paris: Colin, 1993.

Levinas, Emmanuel. *Entre Nous: On Thinking-of-the-Other.* Trans. Michael B. Smith and Barbara Harshav. New York: Columbia University Press, 1998.

Lévy, Bernard-Henri. *La pureté dangereuse.* Paris: Grasset, 1994.

Lipovetsky, Gilles. *Le crépuscule du devoir: L'éthique indolore des nouveaux temps démocratiques.* Paris: Gallimard, 1992.

Luhmann, Niklas. *Love as Passion: The Codification of Intimacy.* Trans. Jeremy Gaines and Doris L. Jones. Cambridge: Harvard University Press, 1986.

Lustiger, Jean-Marie. *Devenez dignes de la condition humaine.* Paris: Flammarion, 1995.

Manson, Tim. "Banalisation du nazisme?" *Le Débat,* September 1982.

Marion, Jean-Luc. *Prolégomènes à la charité.* Paris: Editions de la Différence, 1986.

Morand, Georges. *Sors de cet homme, Satan.* Paris: Fayard, 1993.

Nietzsche, Friedrich. *Twilight of the Idols.* In *The Portable Nietzsche,* ed. and trans. Walter Kaufmann. New York: Viking, 1968.

———. *The Will to Power.* Trans. Walter Kaufmann and R. J. Hollingdale, ed. Walter Kaufmann. New York: Vintage Books, 1967.

Papini, Giovanni. *The Devil.* Trans. Adrienne Foulke. New York: Dutton, 1954.

Philonenko, Alexis. *L'archipel de la conscience européene.* Paris: Grasset, 1990.

Riffault, Hélène. *Les valeurs des Français.* Paris: PUF, 1994.

Rinpoche, Sogyal. *The Tibetan Book of Living and Dying.* San Francisco: Harper San Francisco, 1992.

Rollet, Jacques. "Les croyances des Français." *Études,* October 1995.

Rougemont, Denis de. *Love in the Western World.* Trans. Montgomery Belgion. Rev. ed. New York: Pantheon, 1956.

Rousseau, Jean-Jacques. *Discourse on Inequality.* In *"The First and Second Discourses" Together with the Replies to Critics and "Essay on the Origin of Languages,"* trans. Victor Gourevitch. New York: Harper and Row, 1986.

———. *Emile, or On Education.* Trans. Alan Bloom. New York: Basic Books, 1979.

Ruffin, Jean-Christophe. *L'aventure humanitaire*. Paris: Gallimard, 1994.

Shorter, Edward. *The Making of the Modern Family*. New York: Basic Books, 1975.

Slama, Alain-Gérard. *L'angelisme exterminateur: Essai sur l'ordre morale contemporain*. Paris: Grasset, 1993.

Stendhal [Henri Marie Beyle]. *On Love*. Trans. H. B. V. under the direction of K. Scott-Moncrieff. N.p.: Boni and Liveright, 1927; Universal Library, 1967.

Stoezel, Jean. *Les valeurs du temps présent: Une enquête européene*. Paris: PUF, 1983.

Taylor, Charles. *Le malaise de la modernité*. Paris: Cerf, 1994.

Todorov, Tzvetan. *Frêle bonheur: Essai sur Rousseau*. Paris: Hachette, 1985.

Trevor-Roper, Hugh. *From Counter-Reformation to Glorious Revolution*. Chicago: University of Chicago Press, 1992.

Weber, Olivier. *French Doctors*. Paris: Laffont, 1995.

Weil, Simone. *Gravity and Grace*. Trans. Arthur Wills. New York: Putnam's, 1952.

Wilson, James Q. *The Moral Sense*. New York: Free Press, 1993.

Yonnet, Daniel, and Louis Costel, *Le diable et l'exorciste*. Rennes: Éditions Ouest-France, 1993.

INDEX